Cat Mandalas Adult Coloring Book Vol 2

60 Entertaining Stress Relieving Cat Patterns

By Omar Johnson

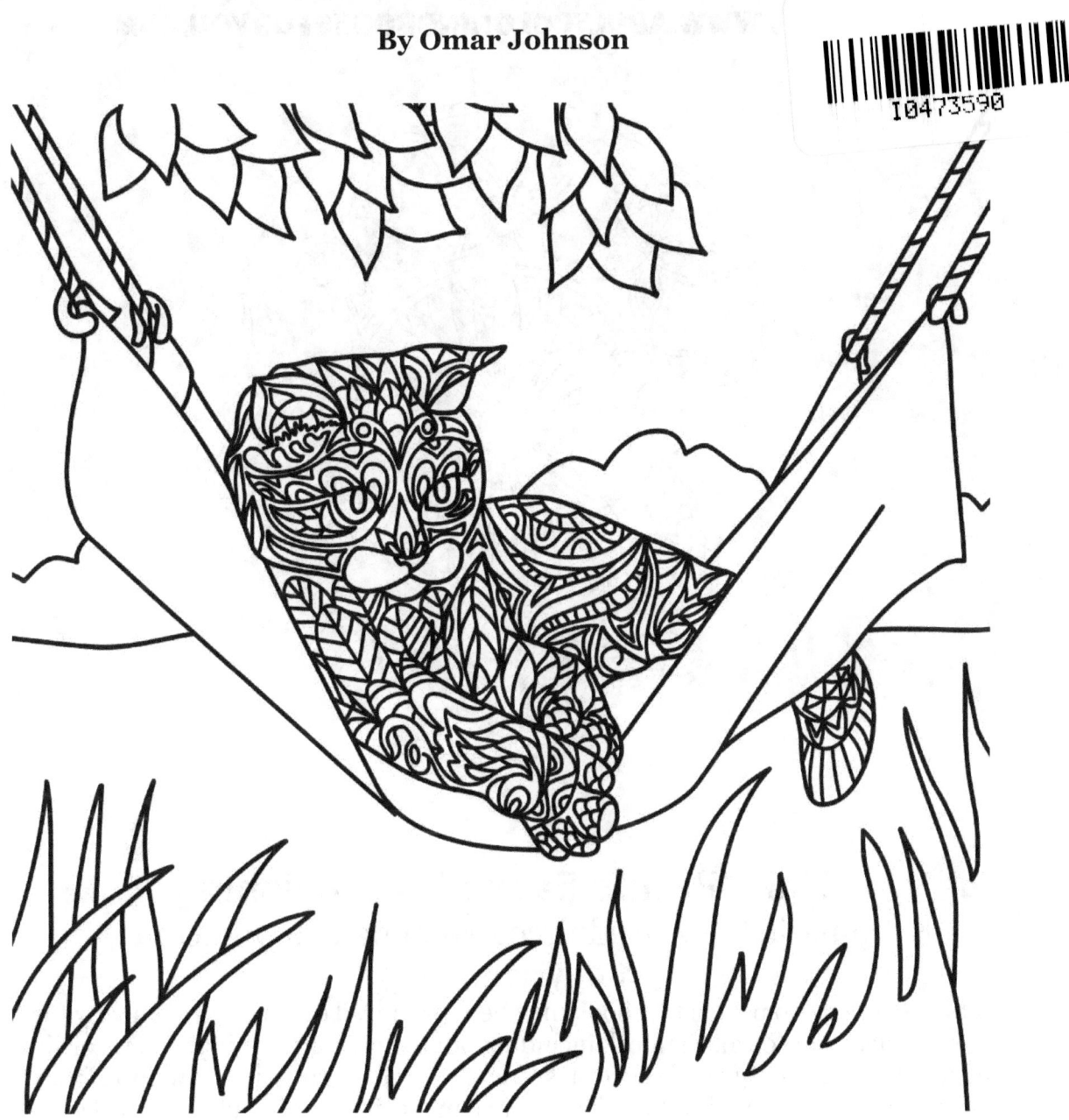

Get Your Free Butterfly Mandala Coloring Book

Visit

HTTPS://WWW.ADULTCOLORINGBOOKSFORYOU.COM

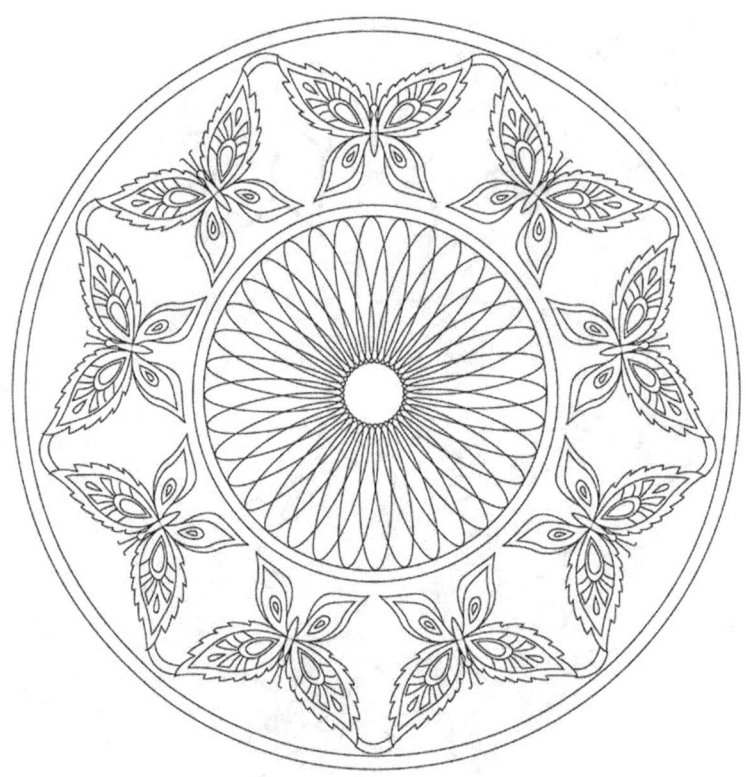

Make Profits Easy LLC Publishing

omarjohnson@adultcoloringbooksforyou.com

Copyright 2019

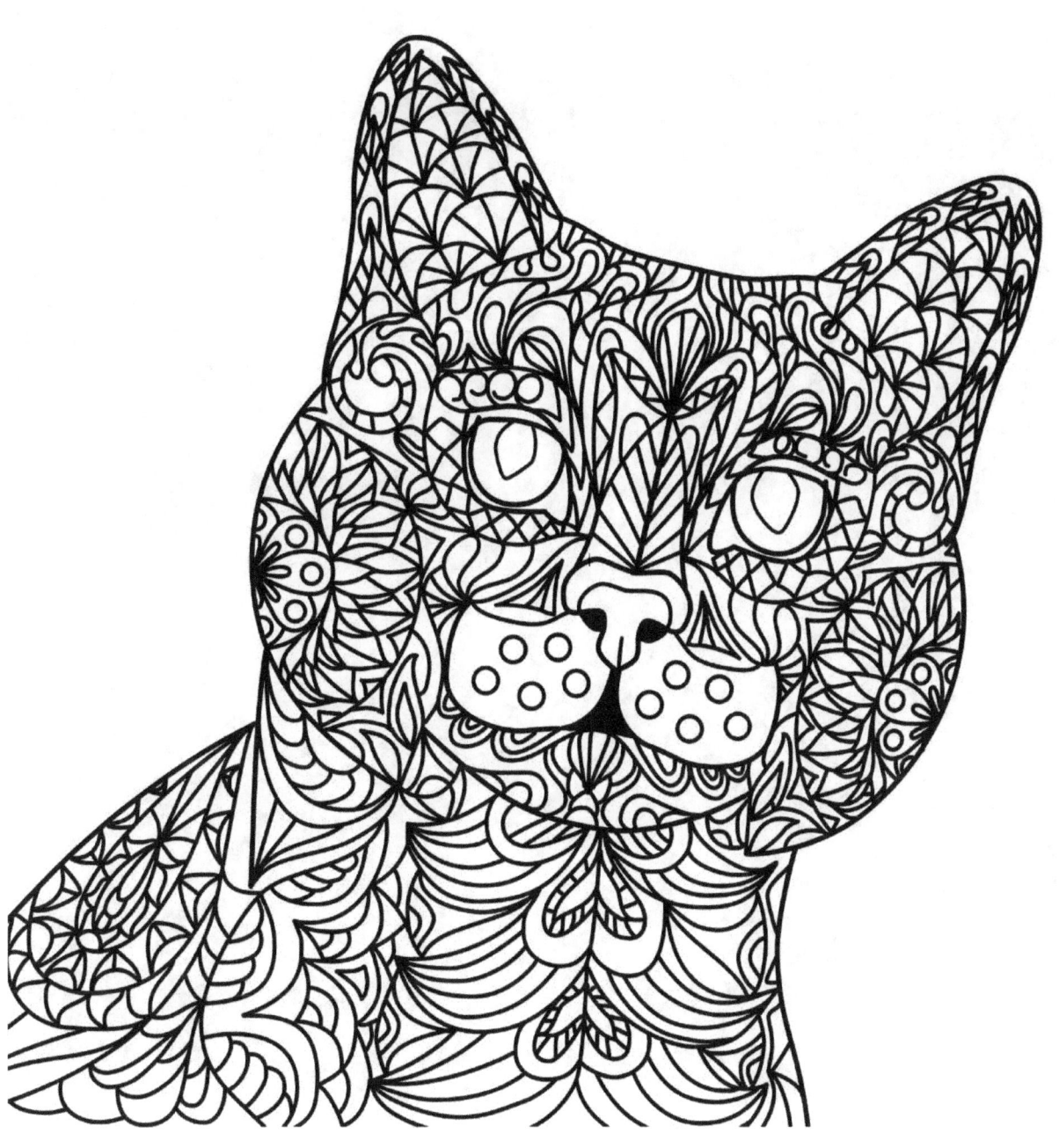

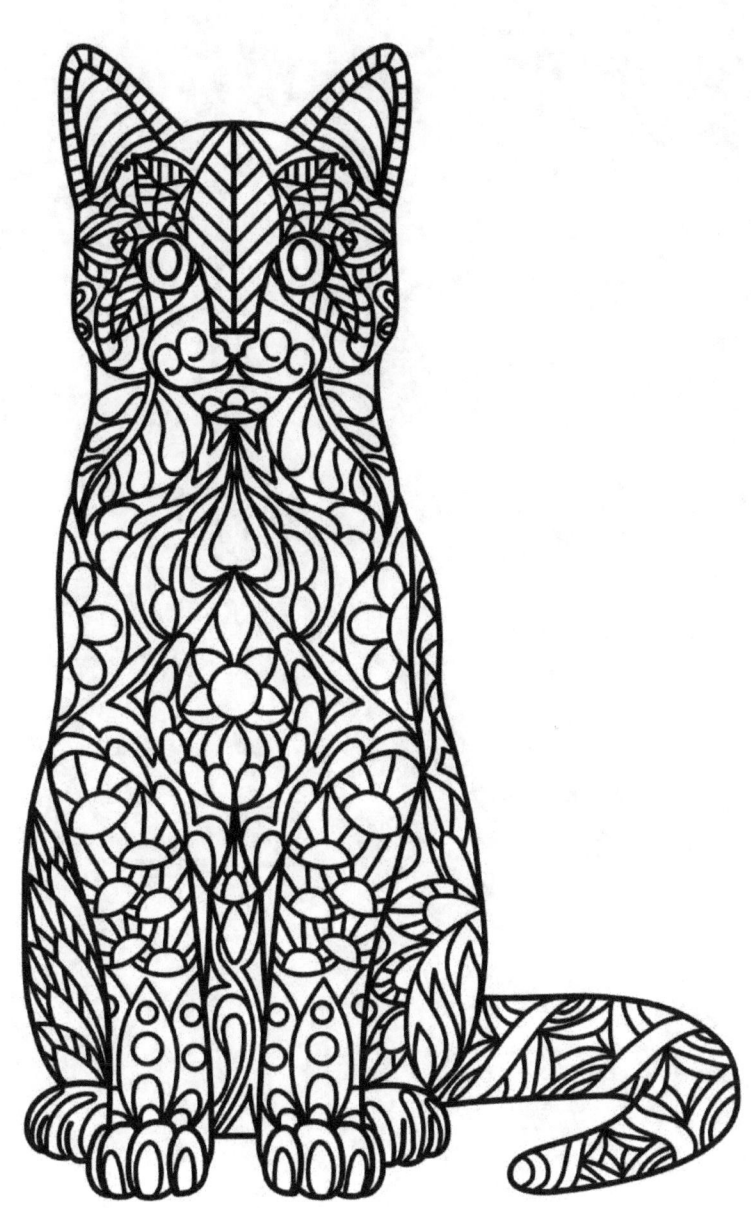

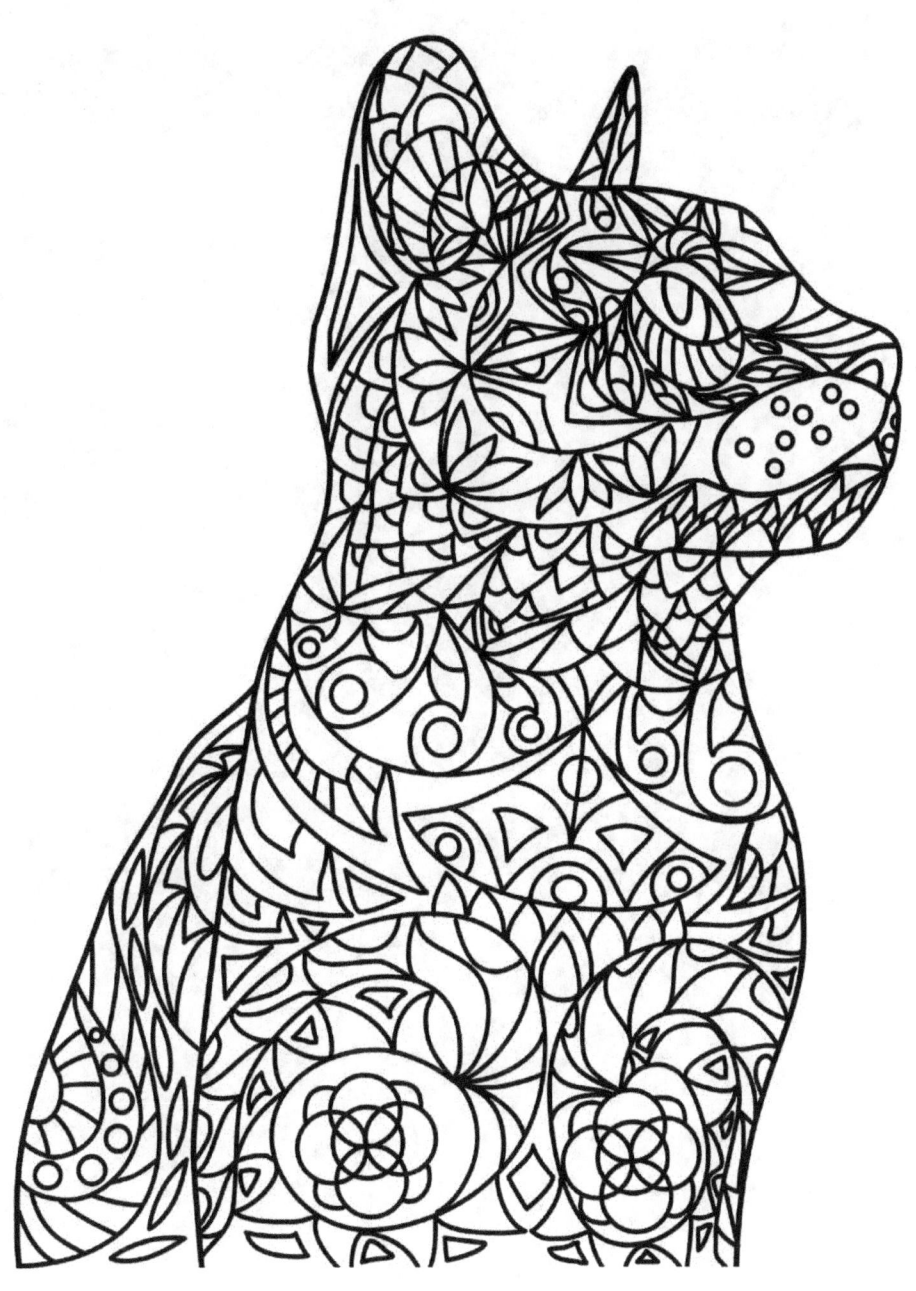

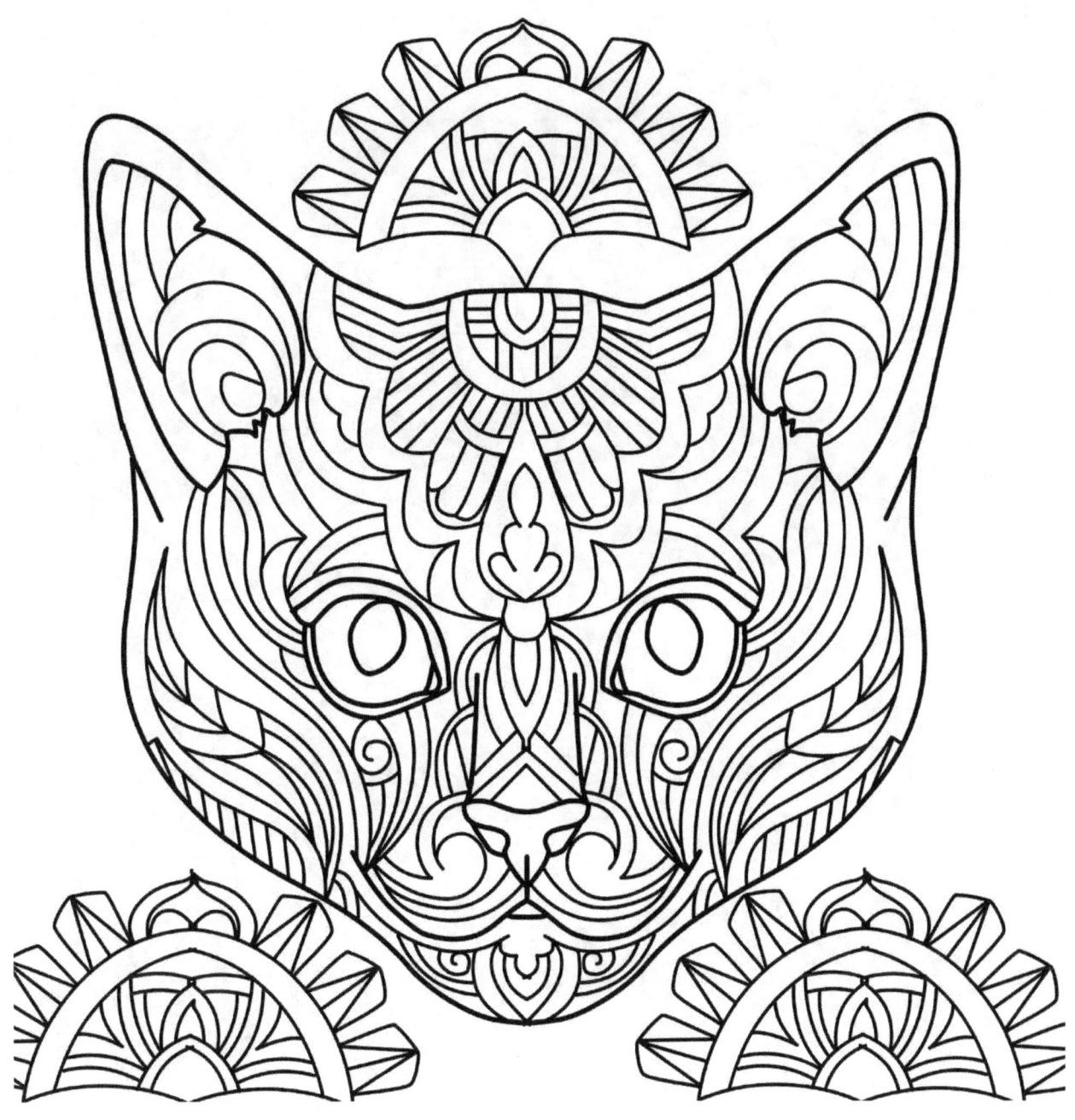

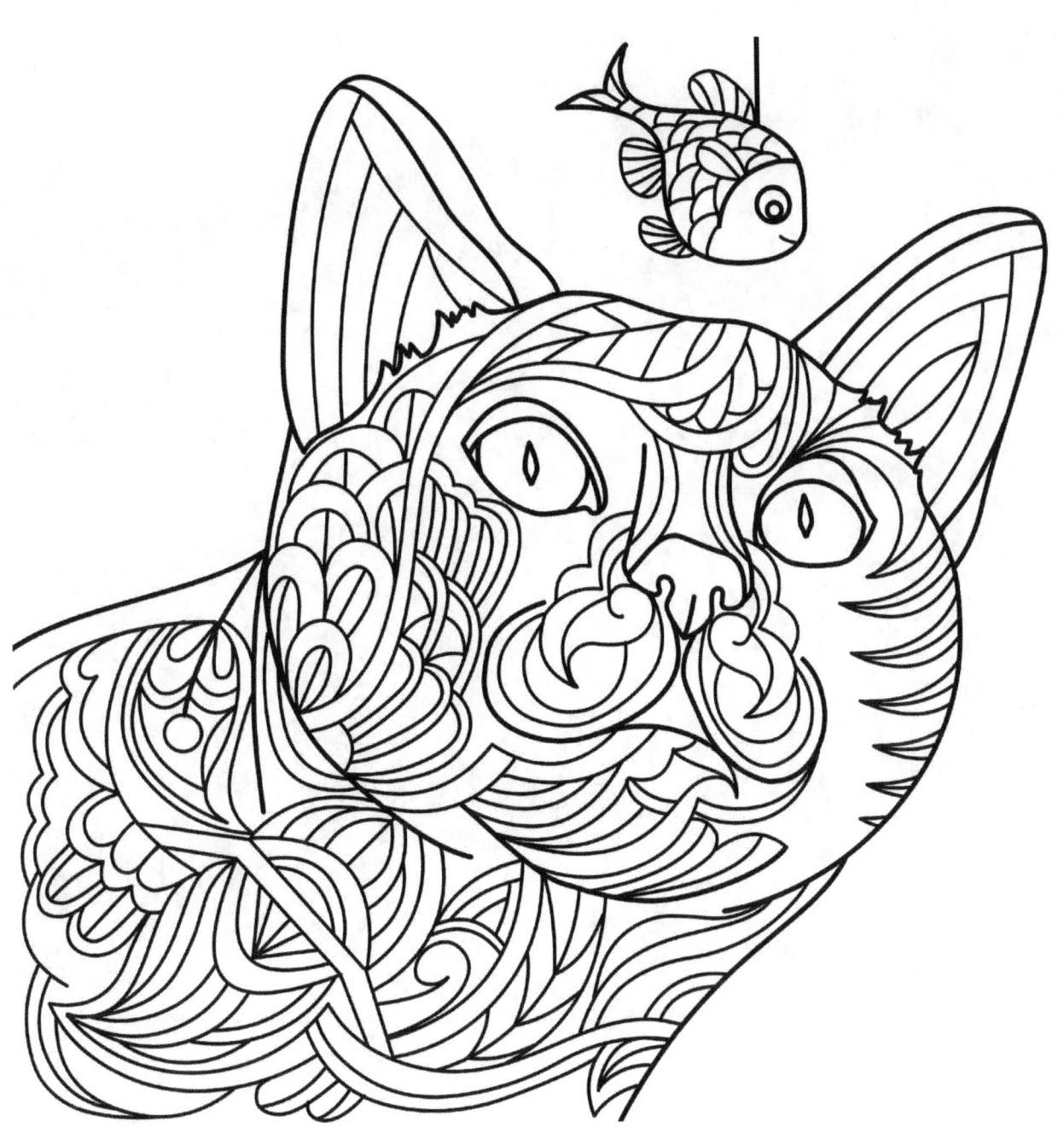

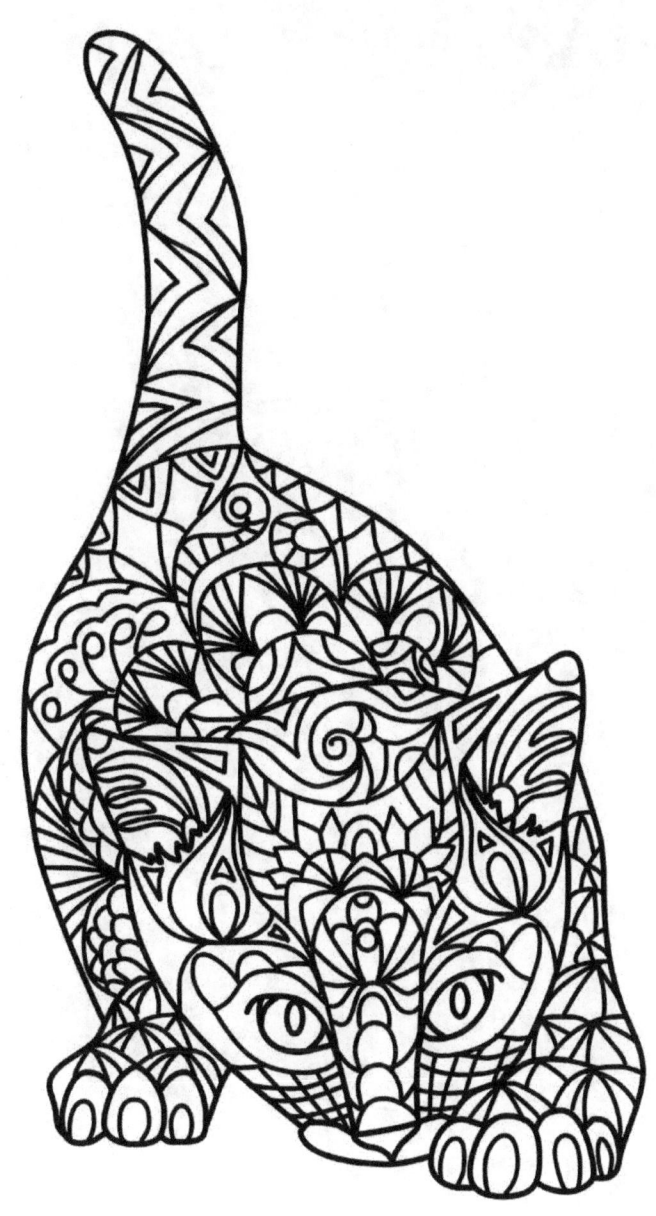

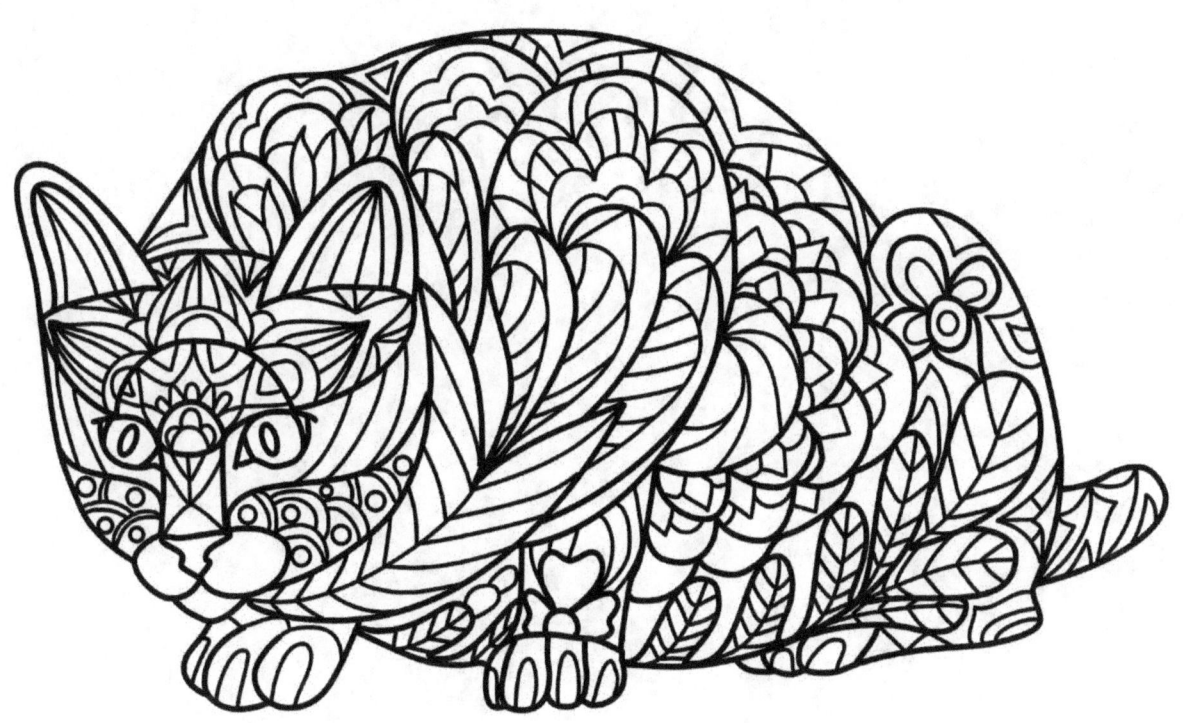

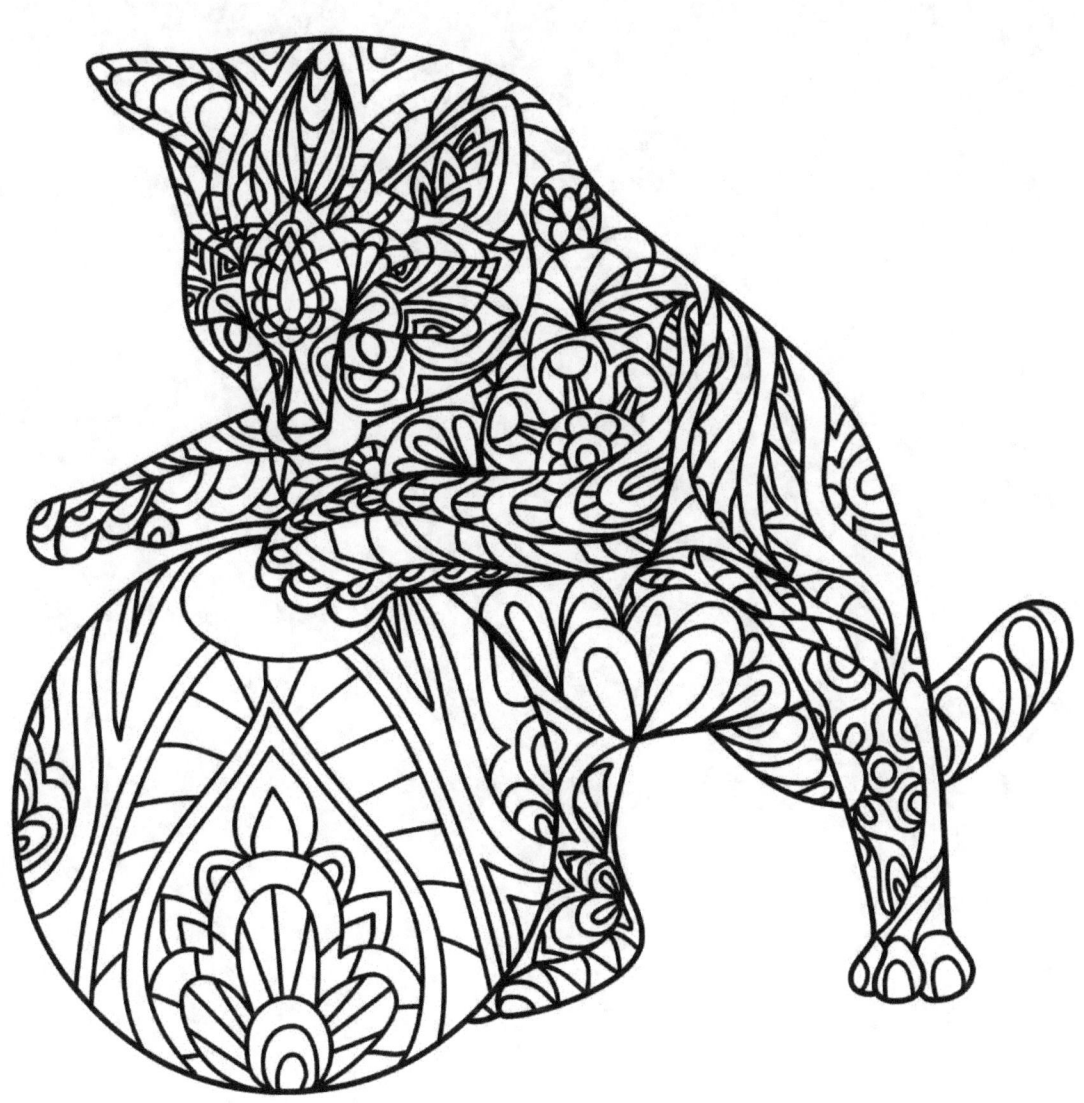

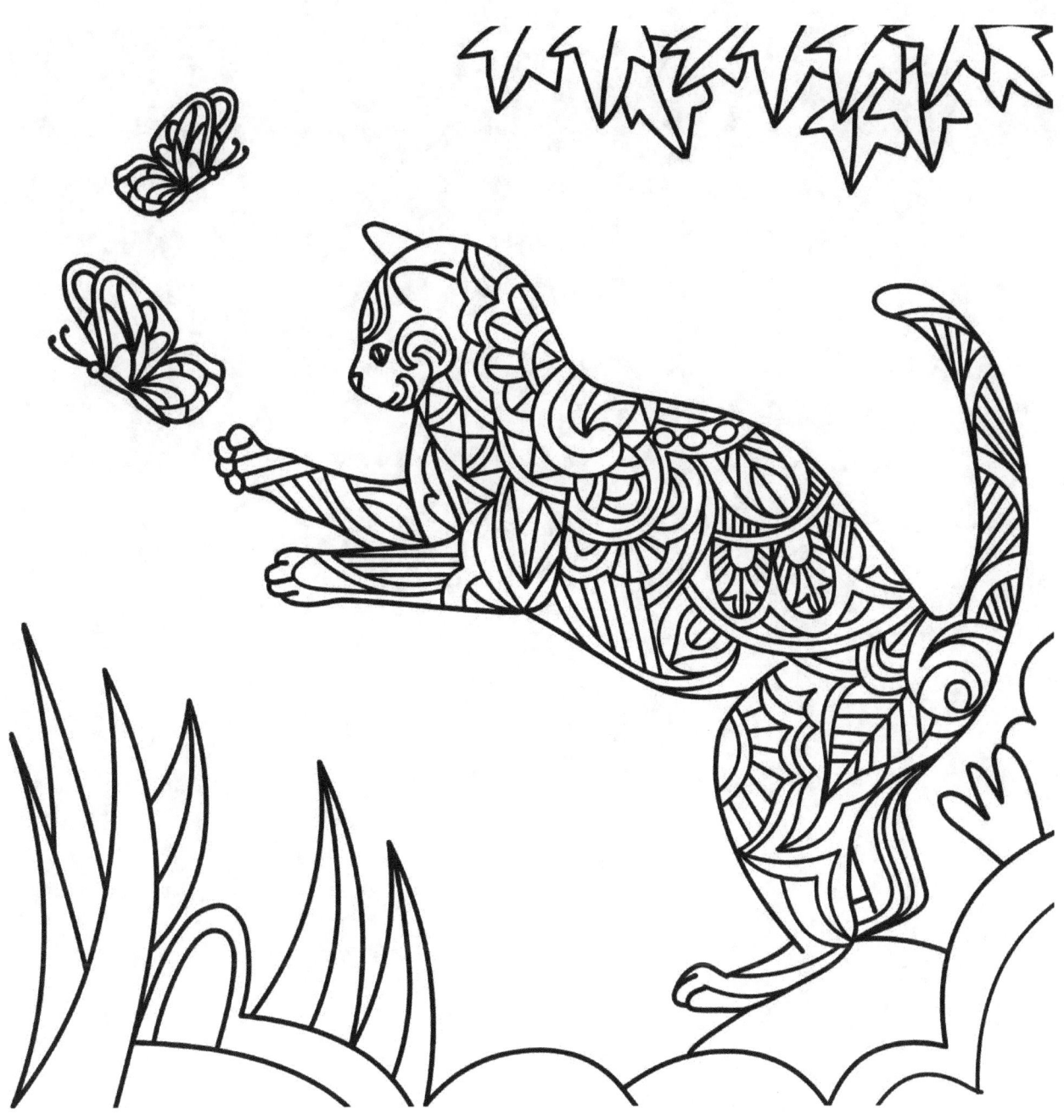

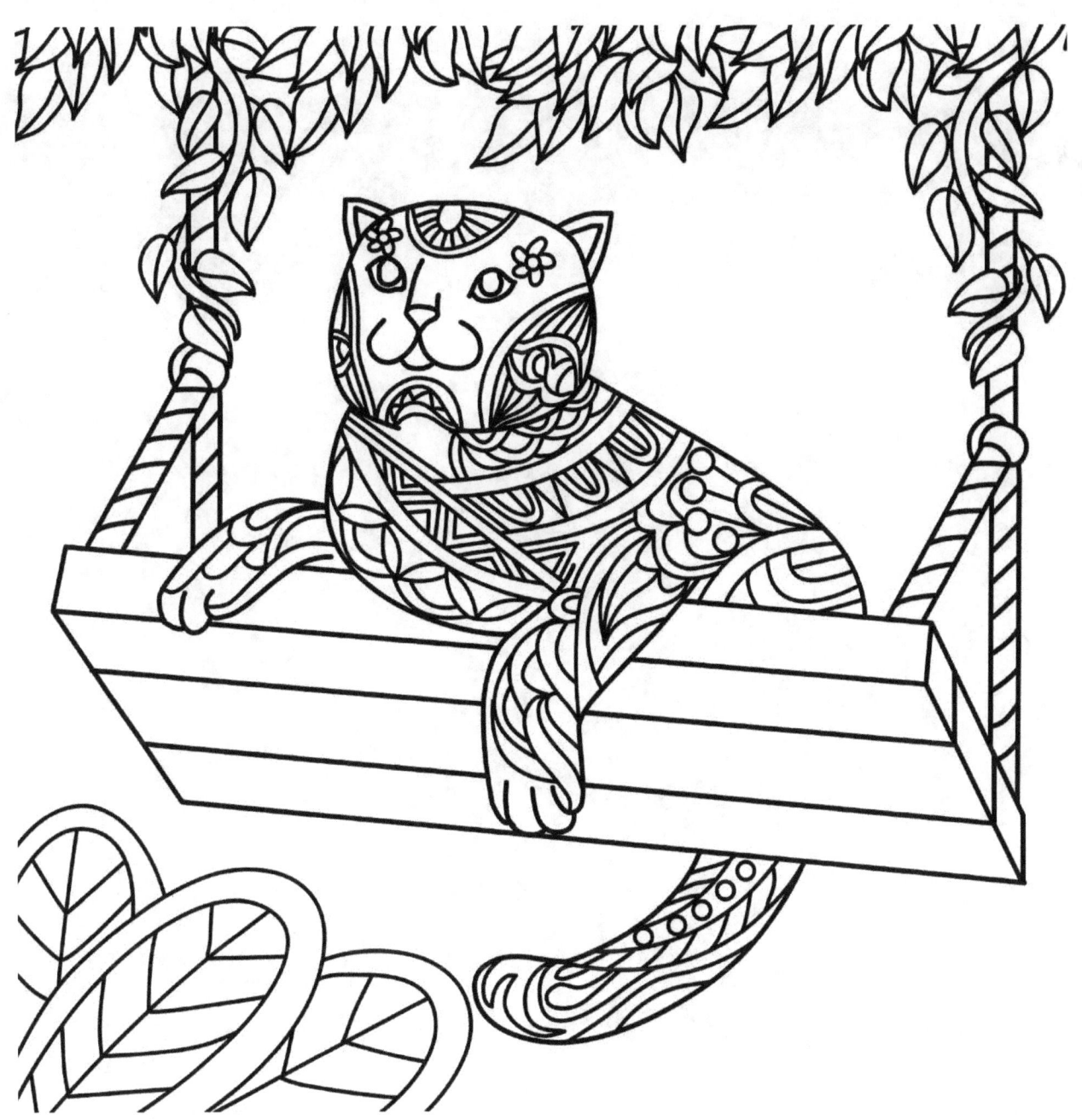

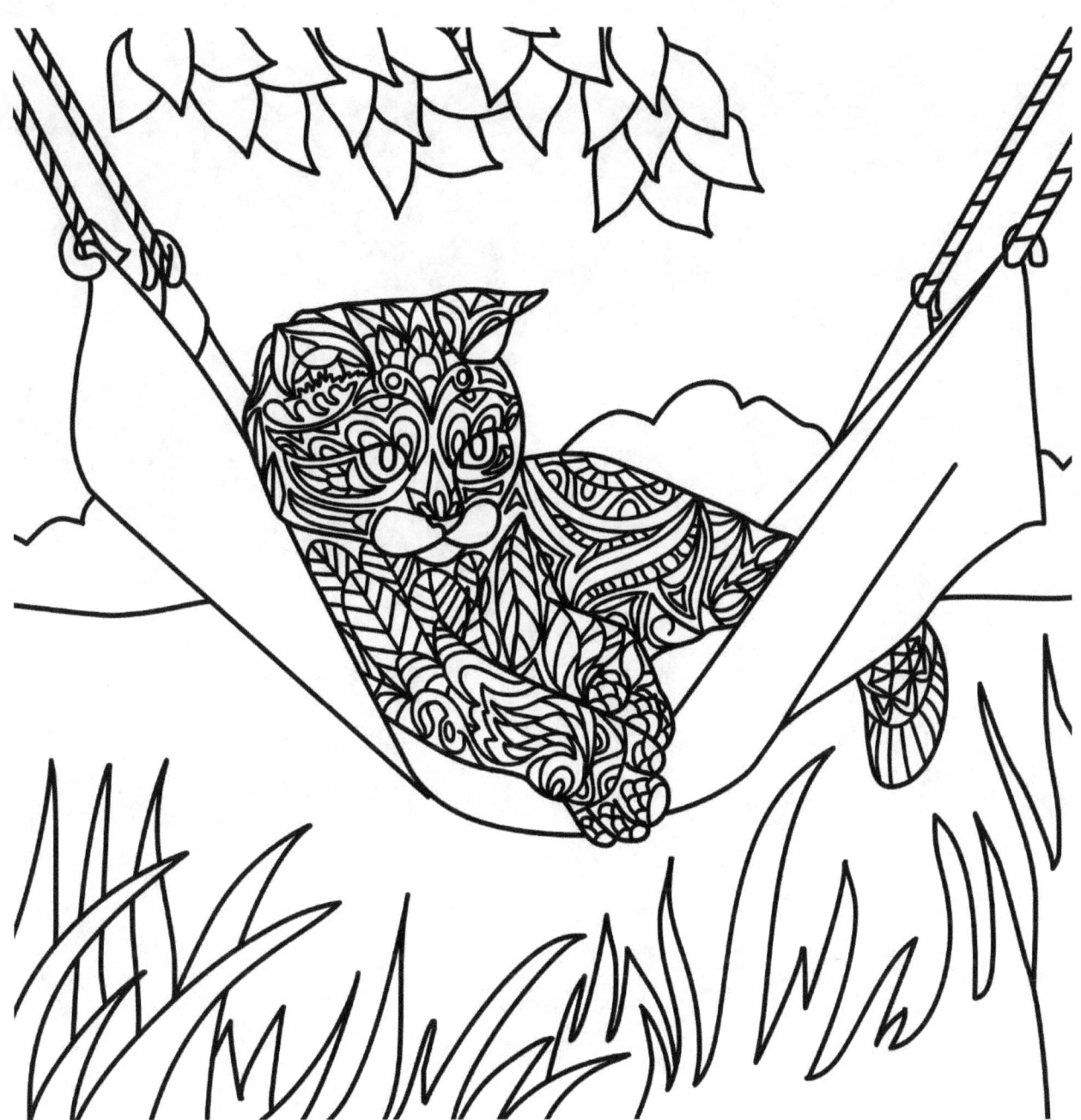

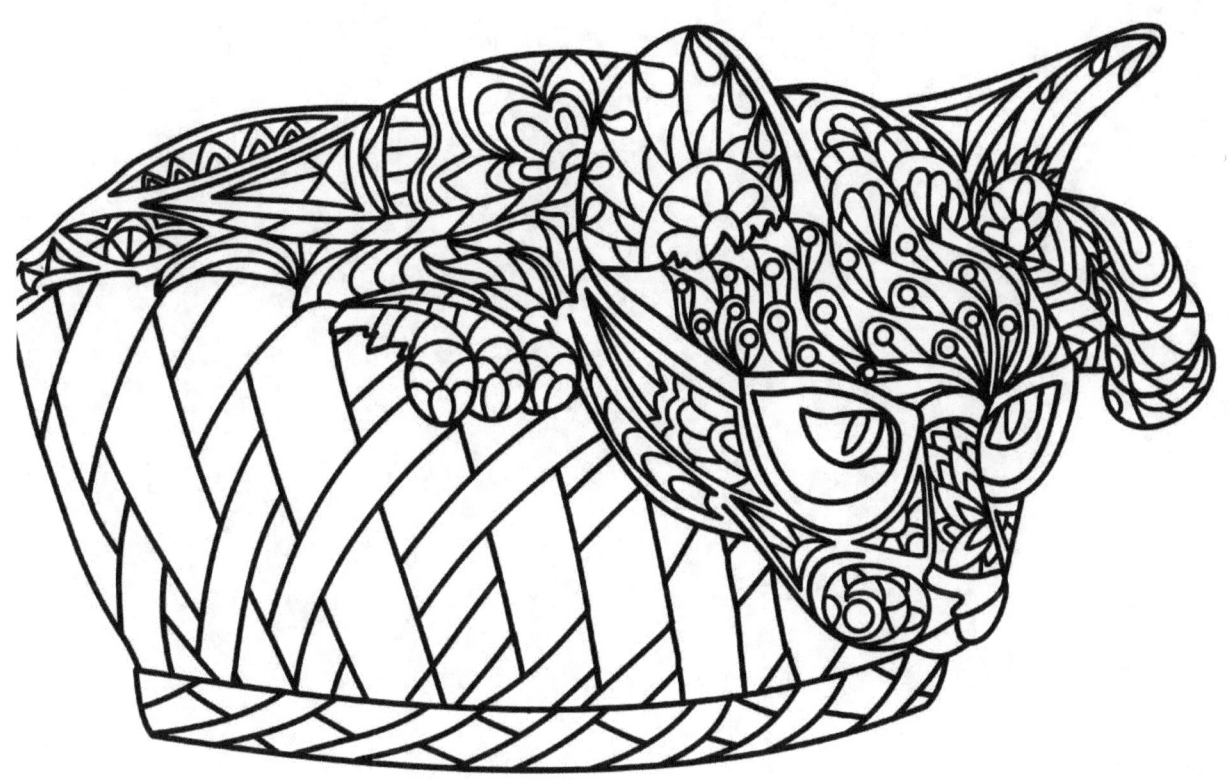

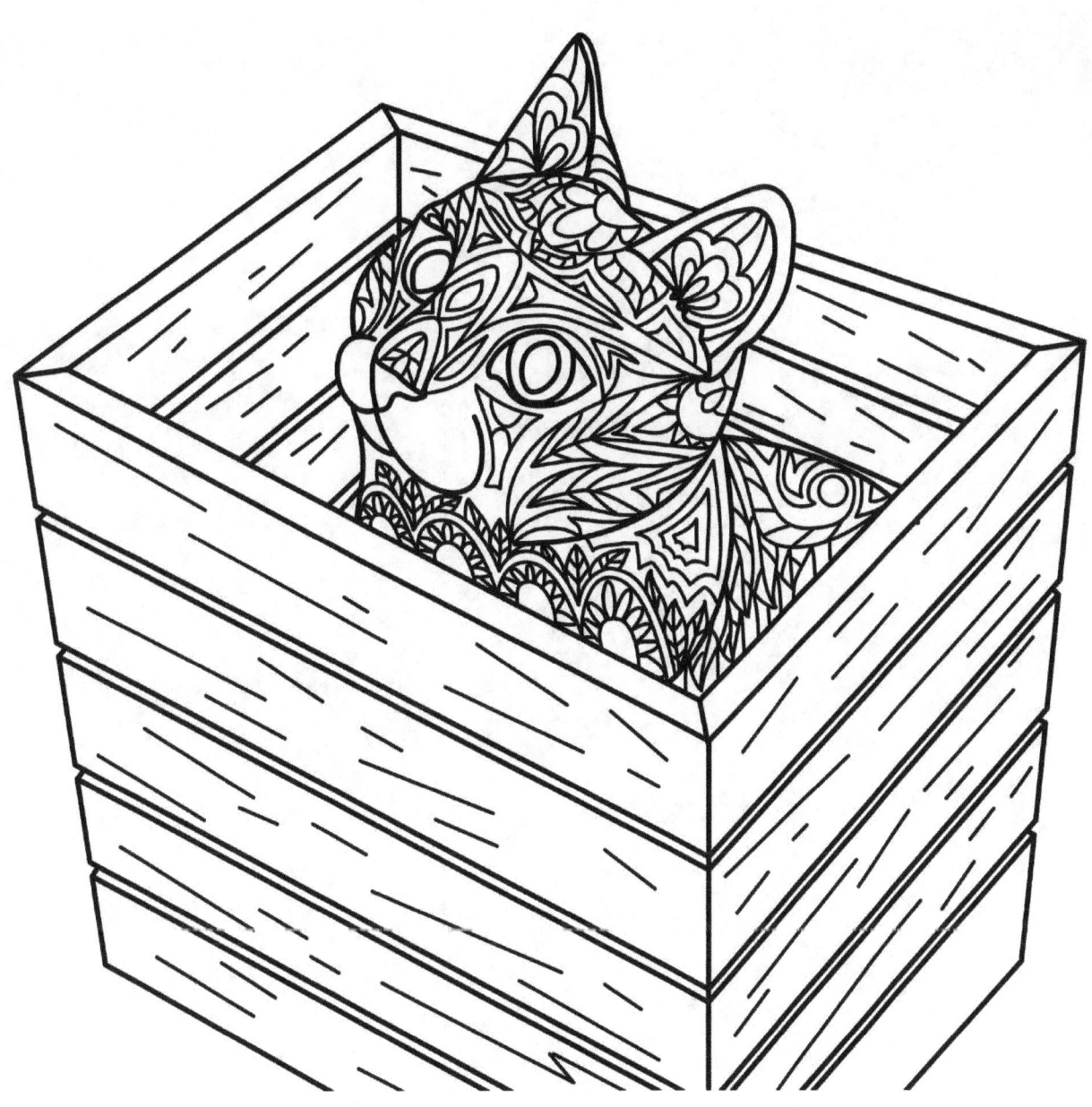

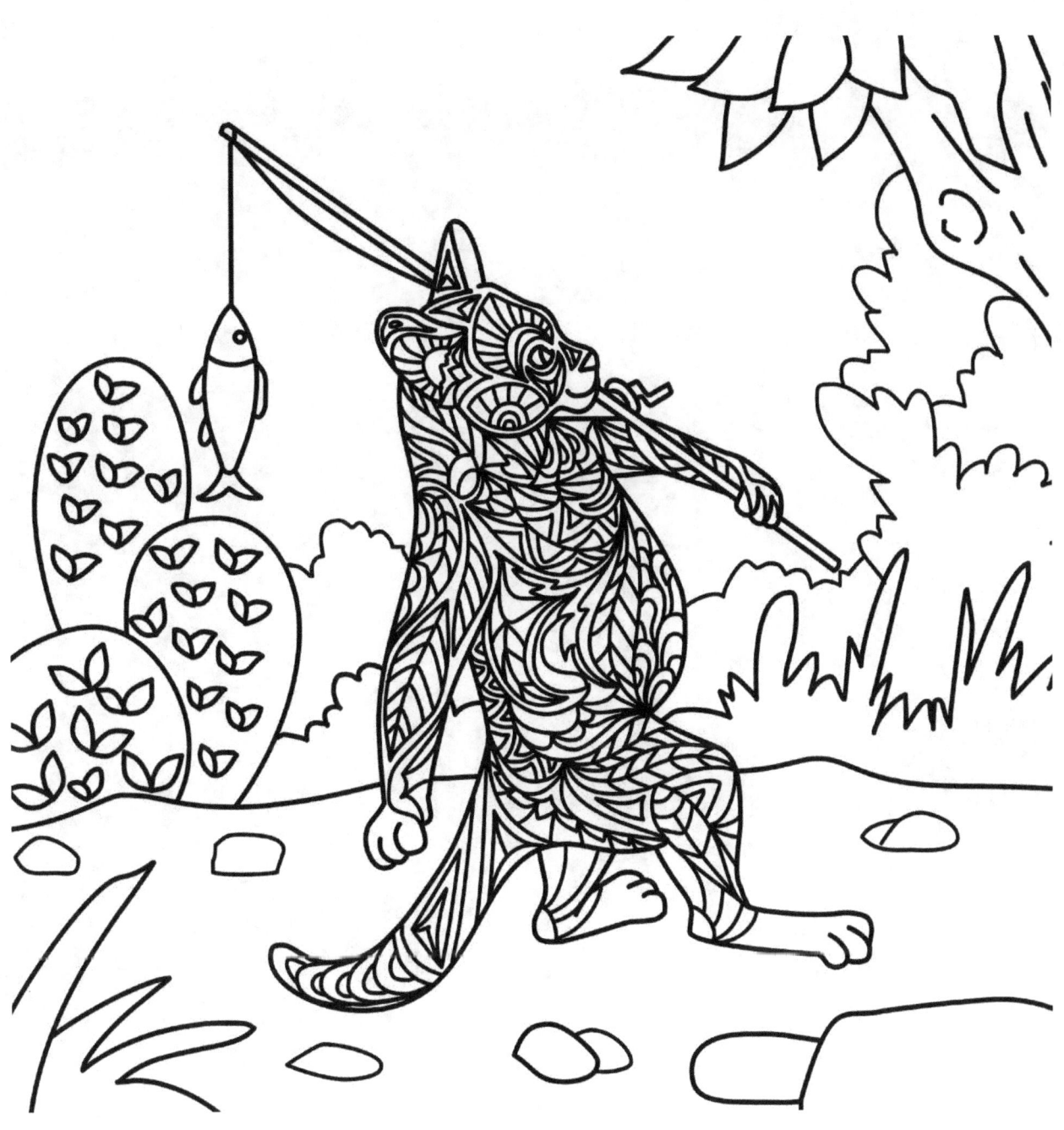

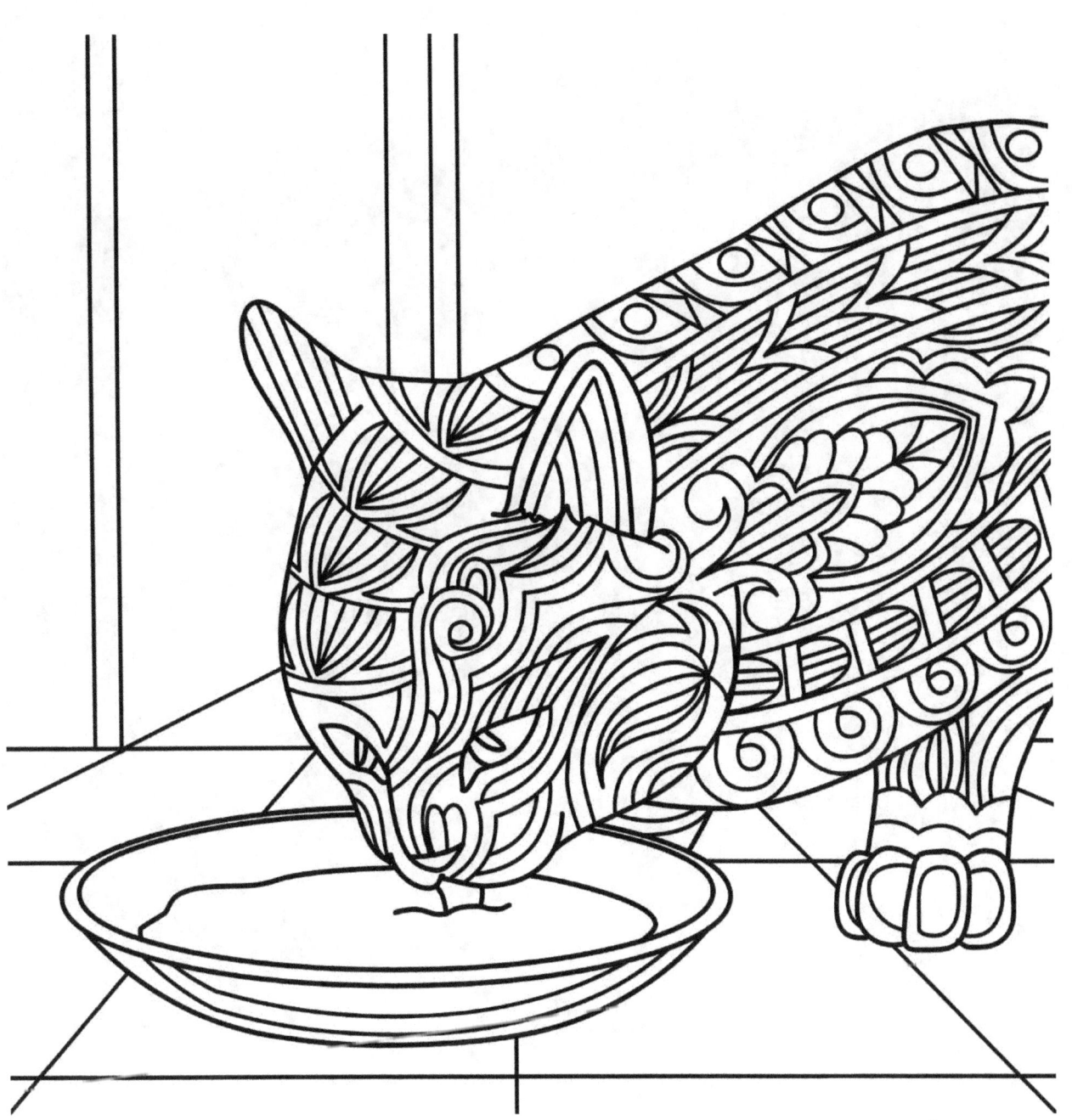

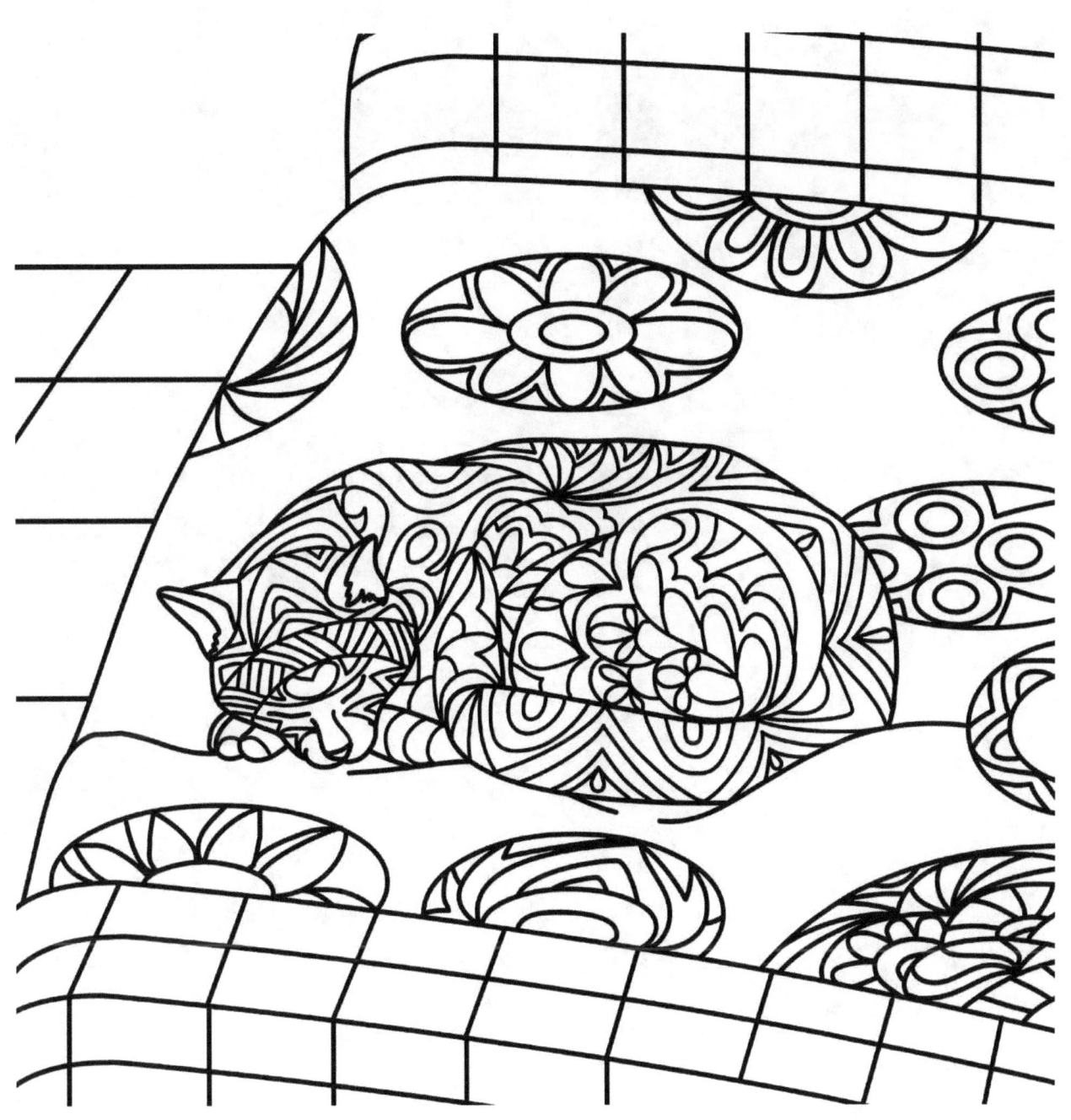

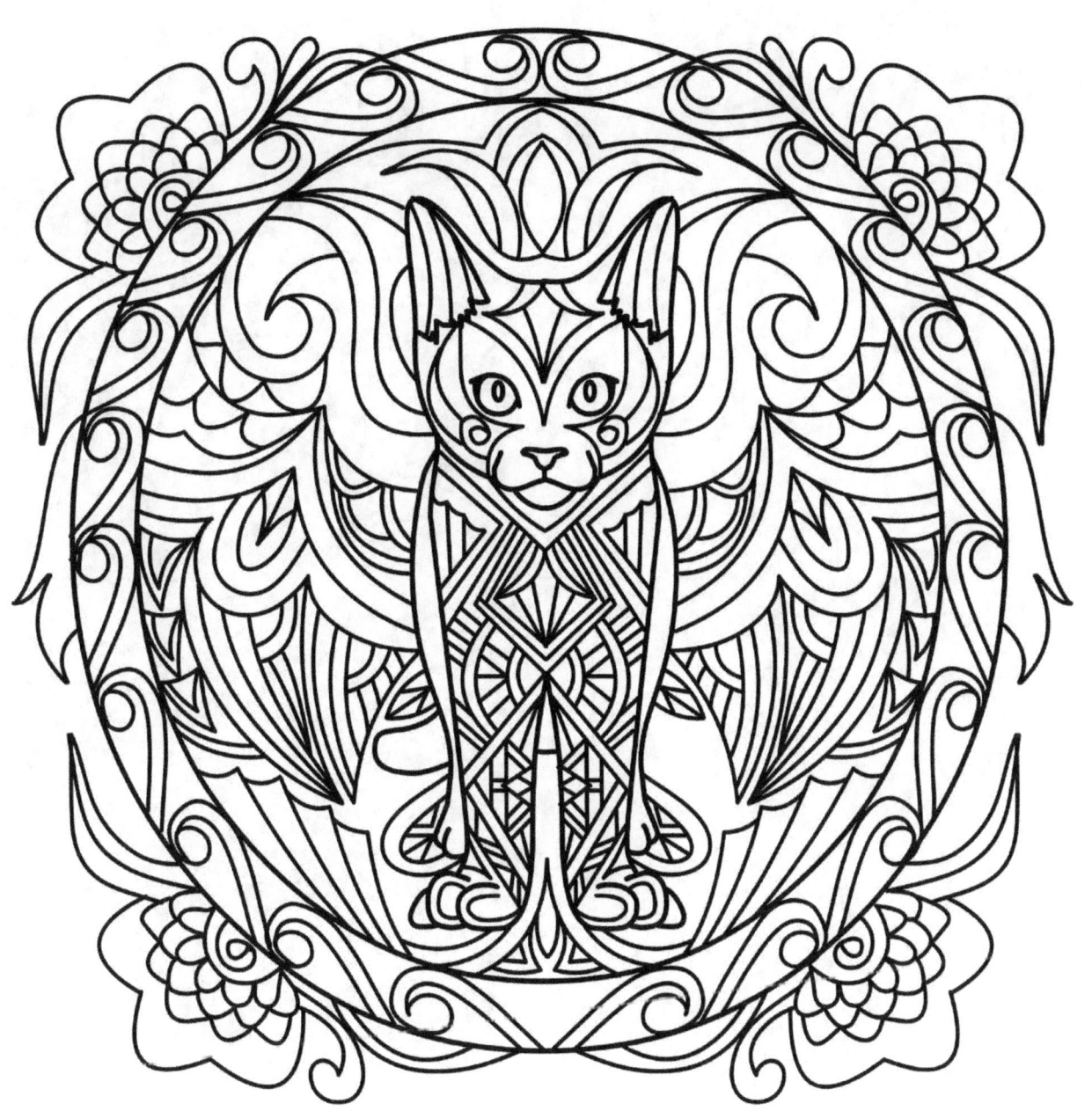

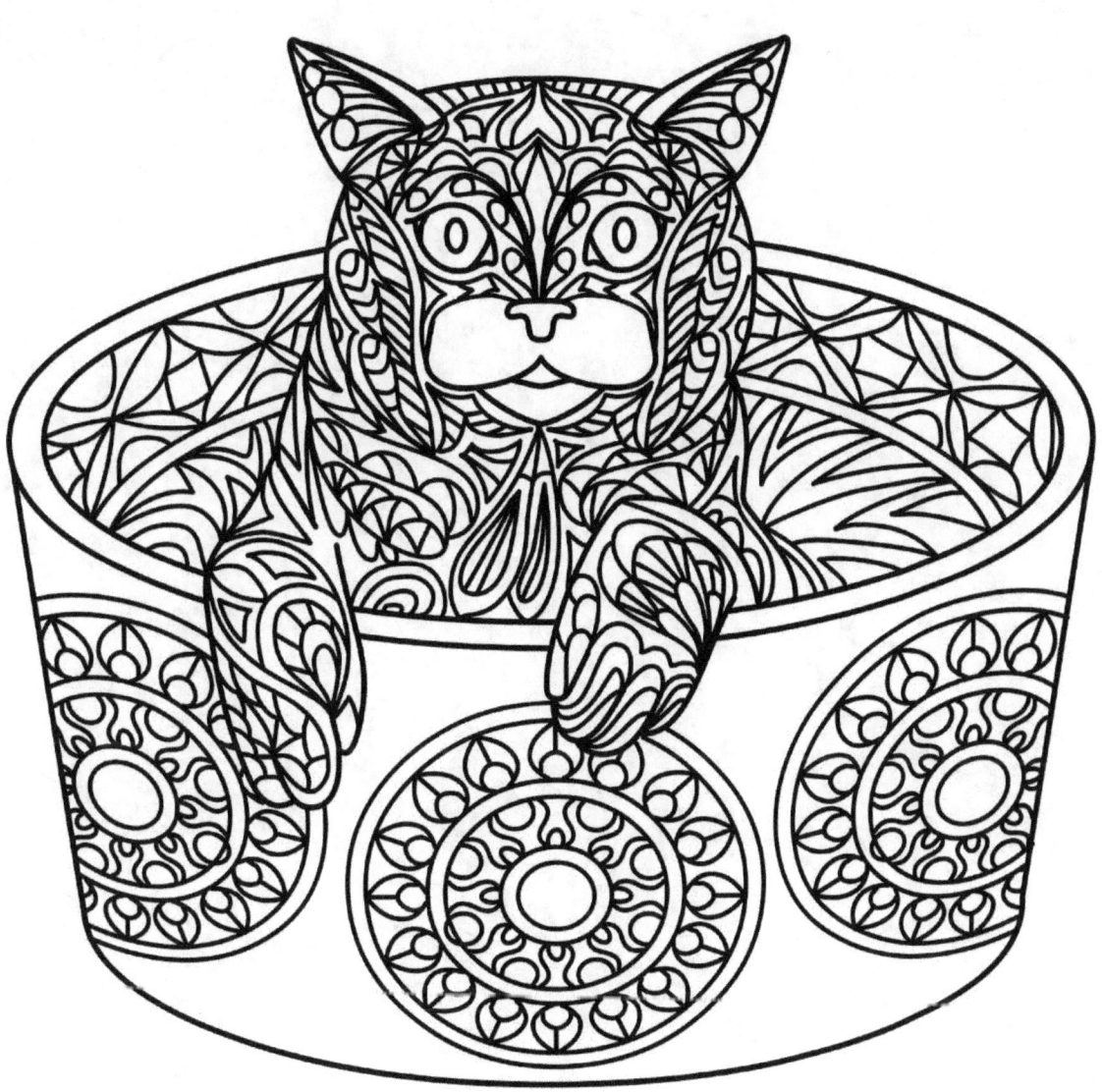

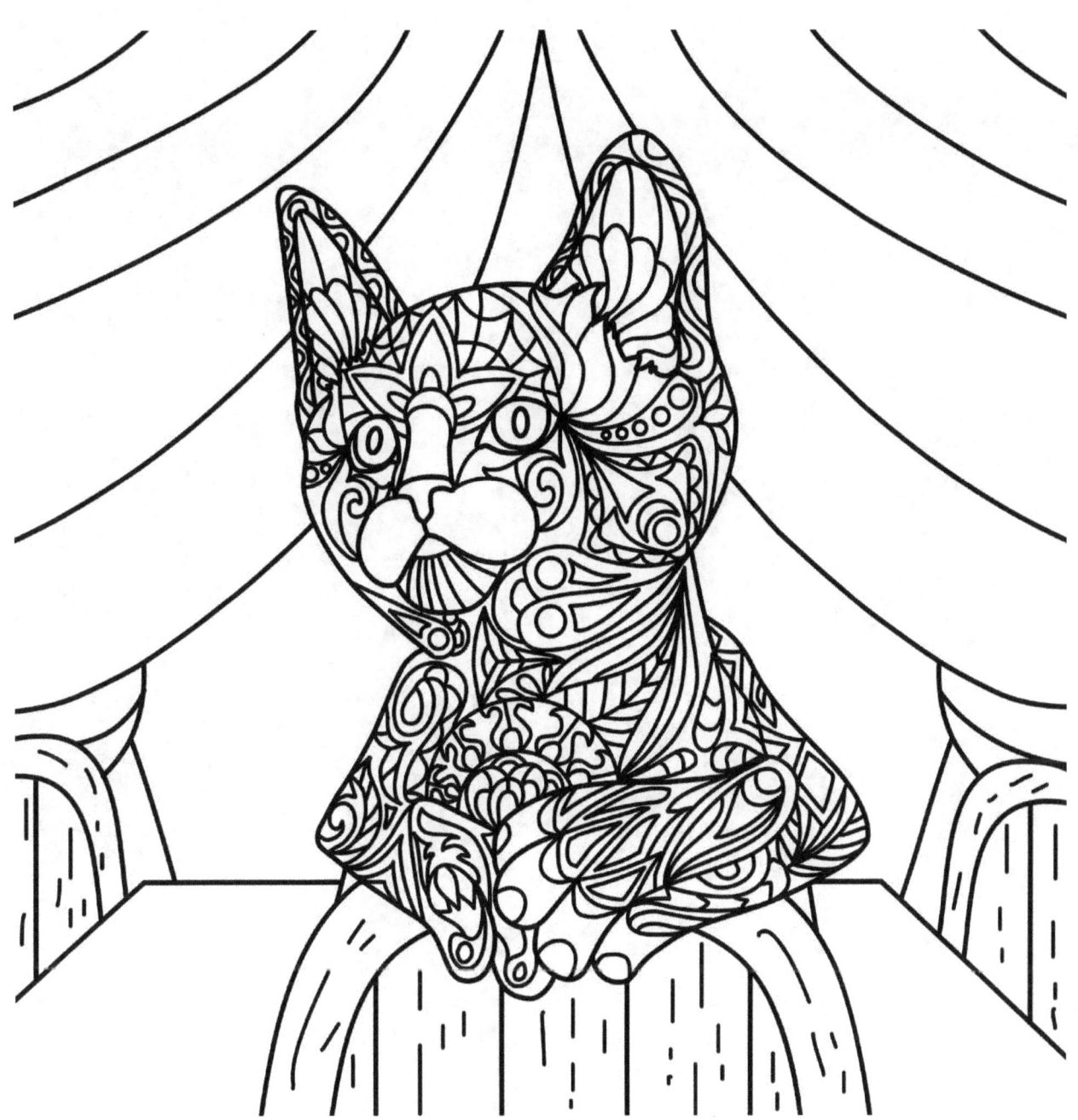

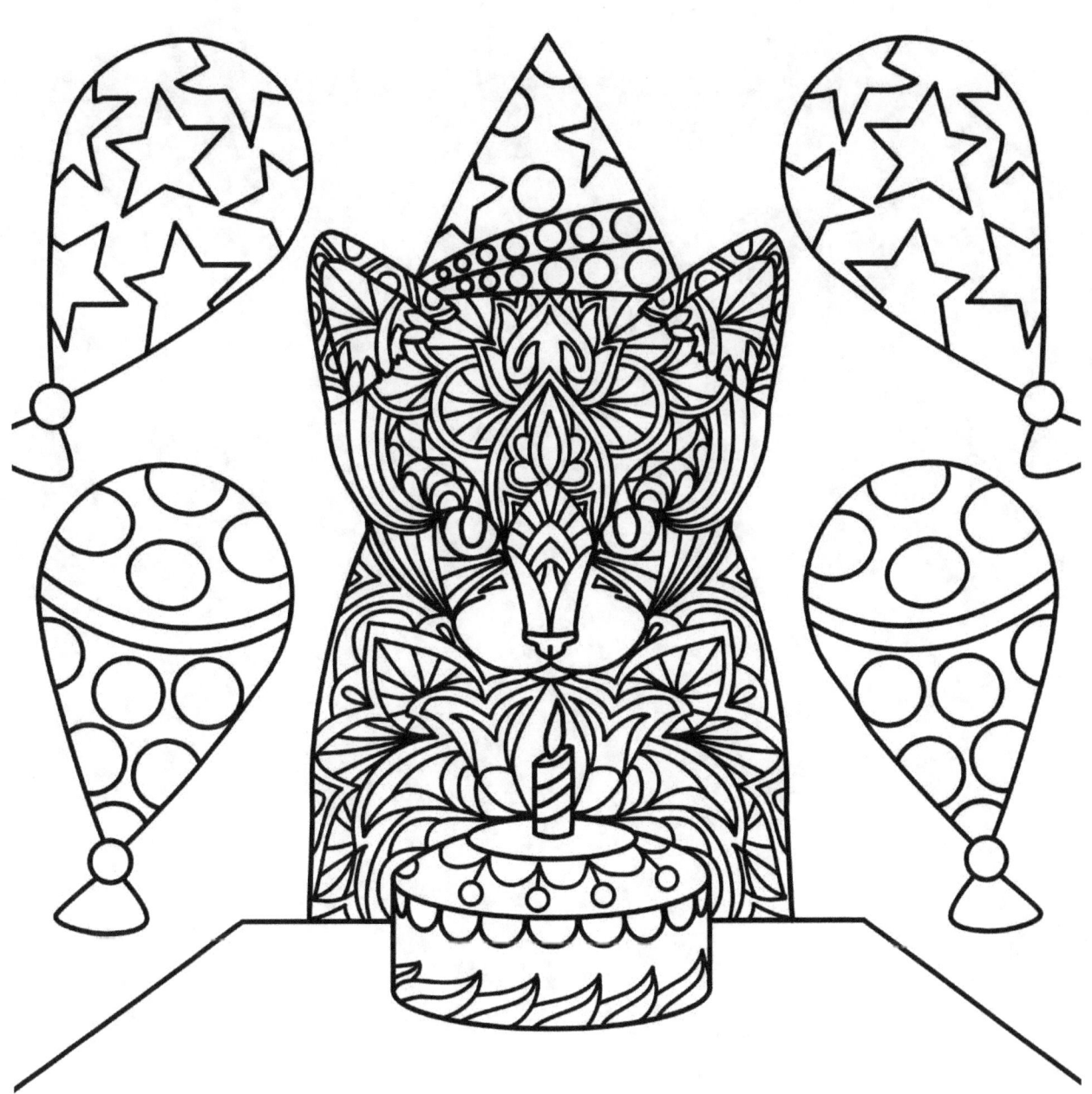

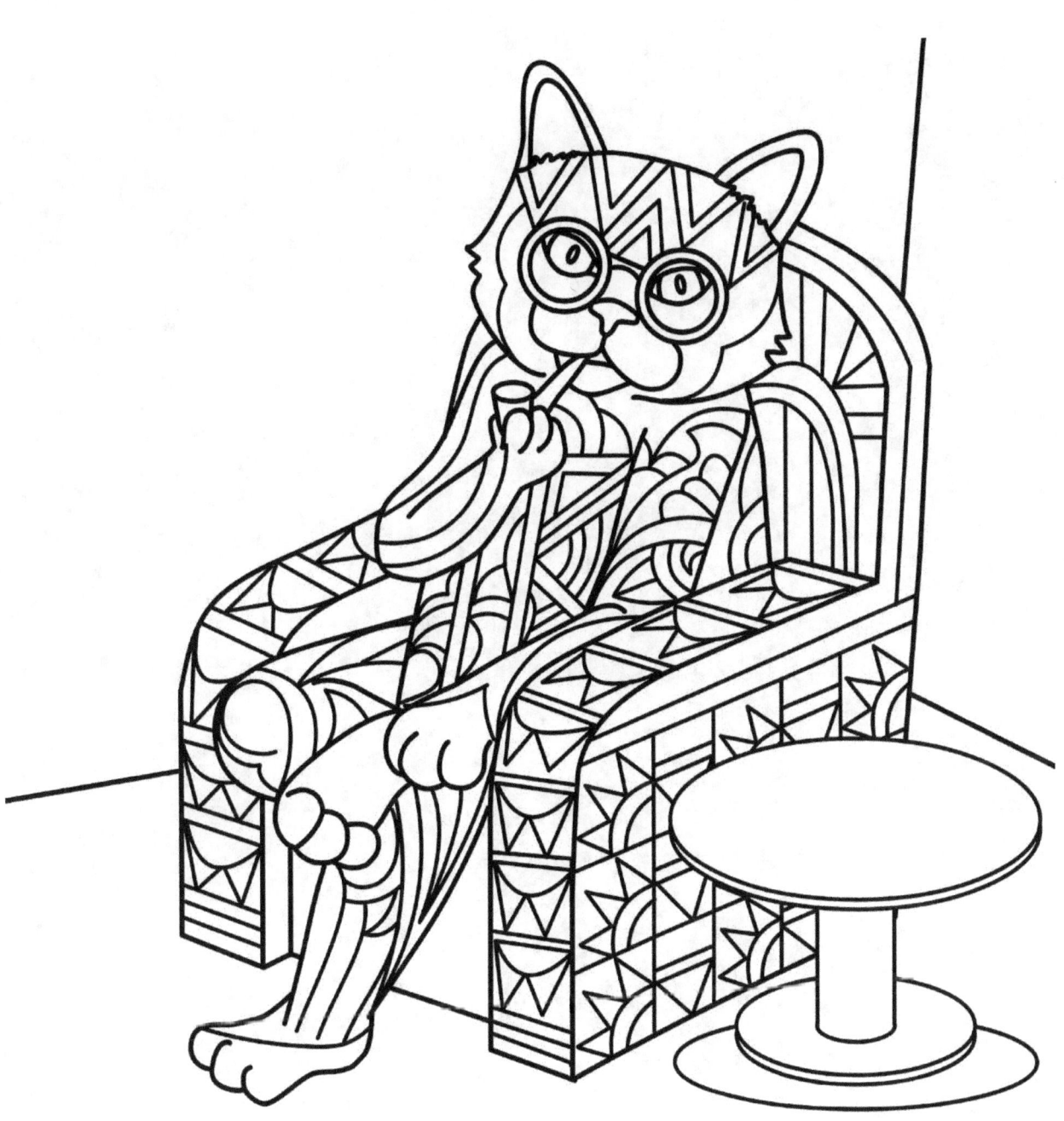

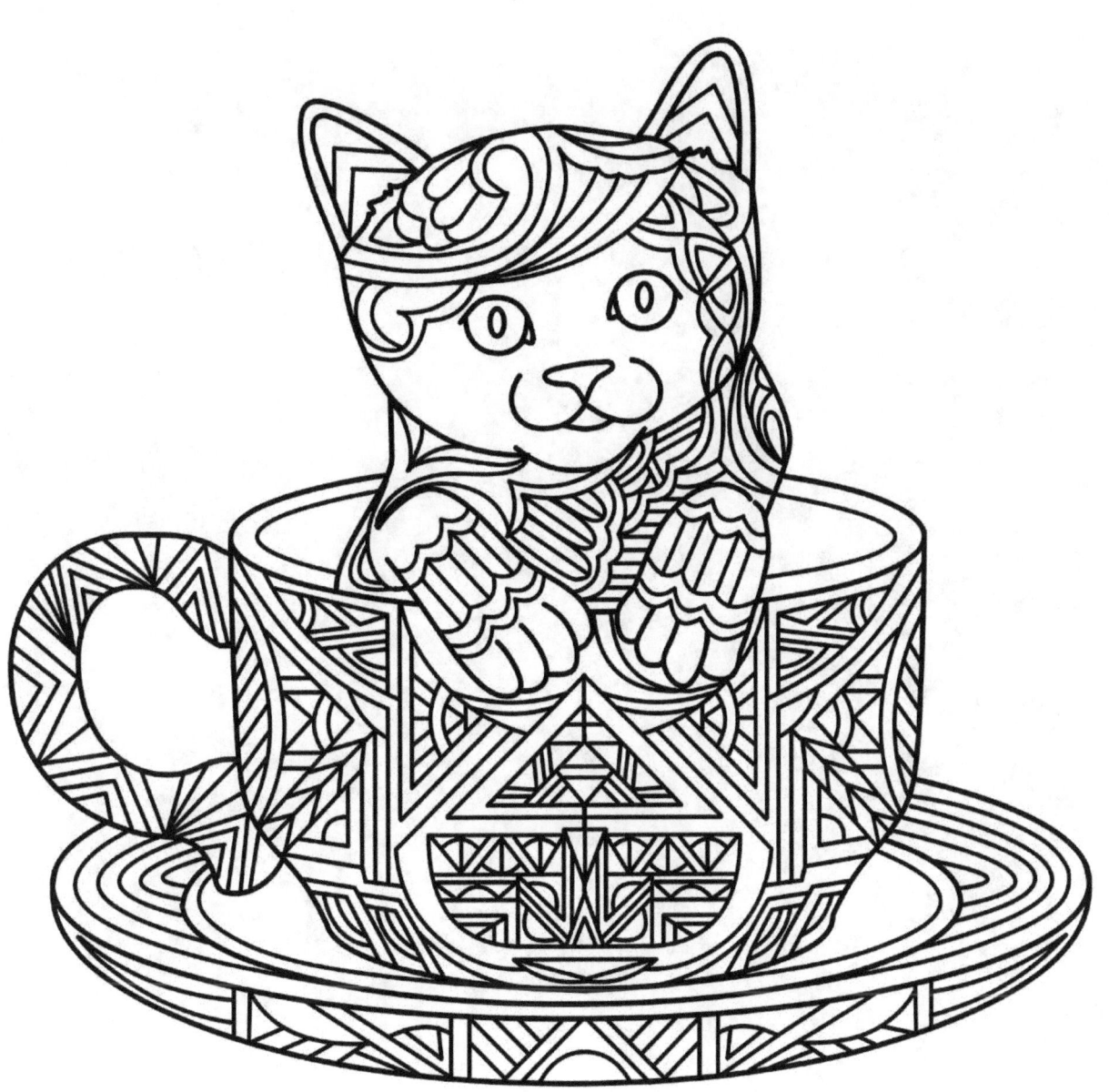

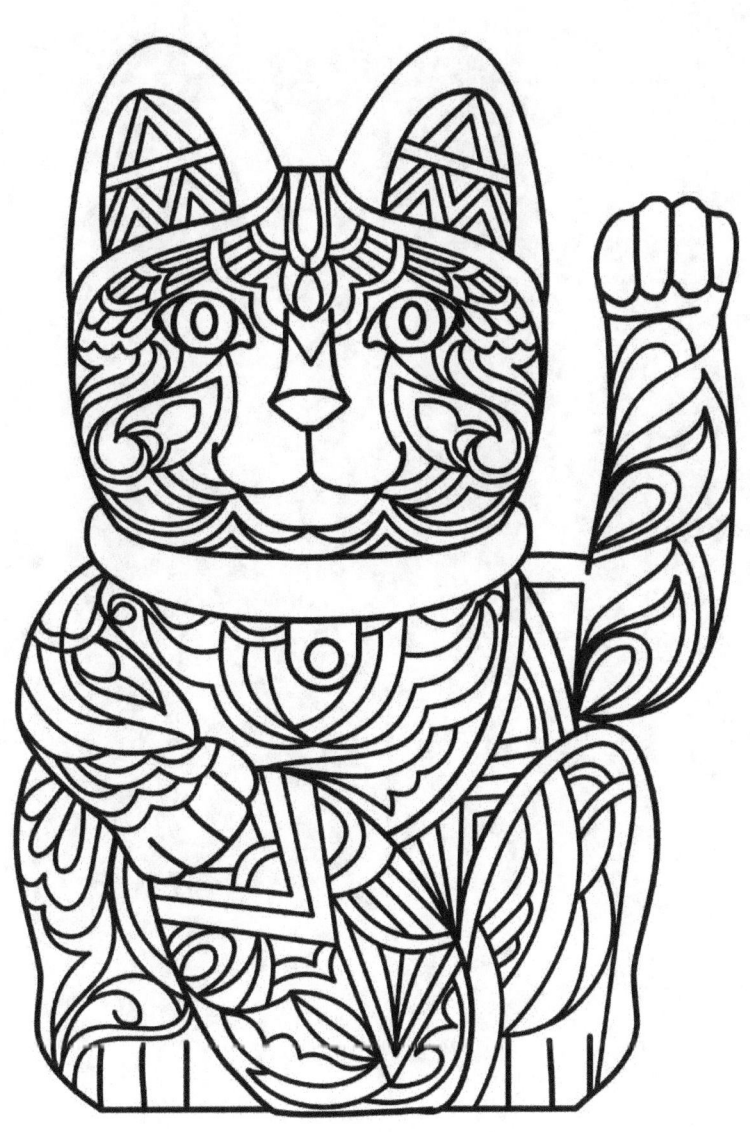

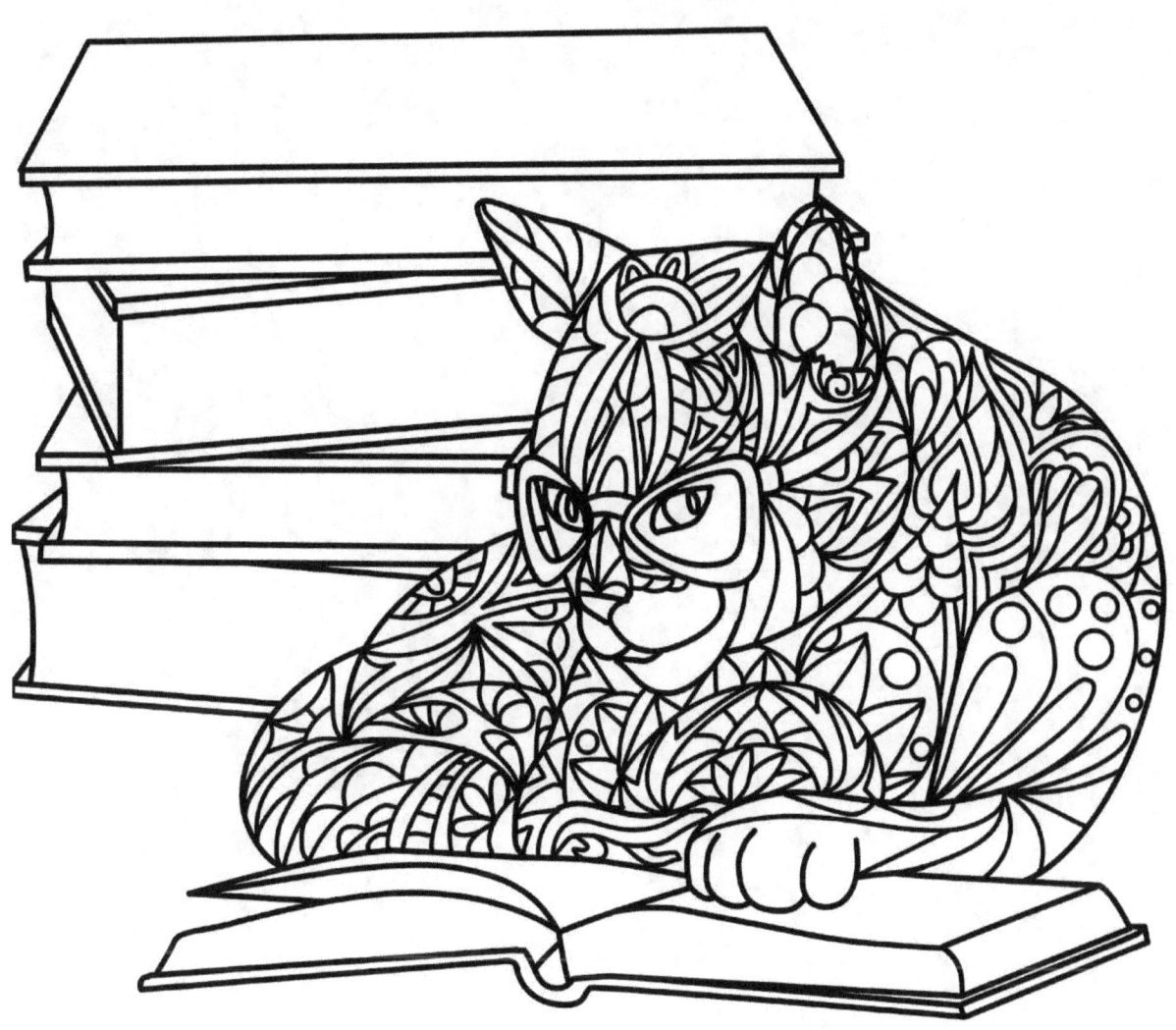

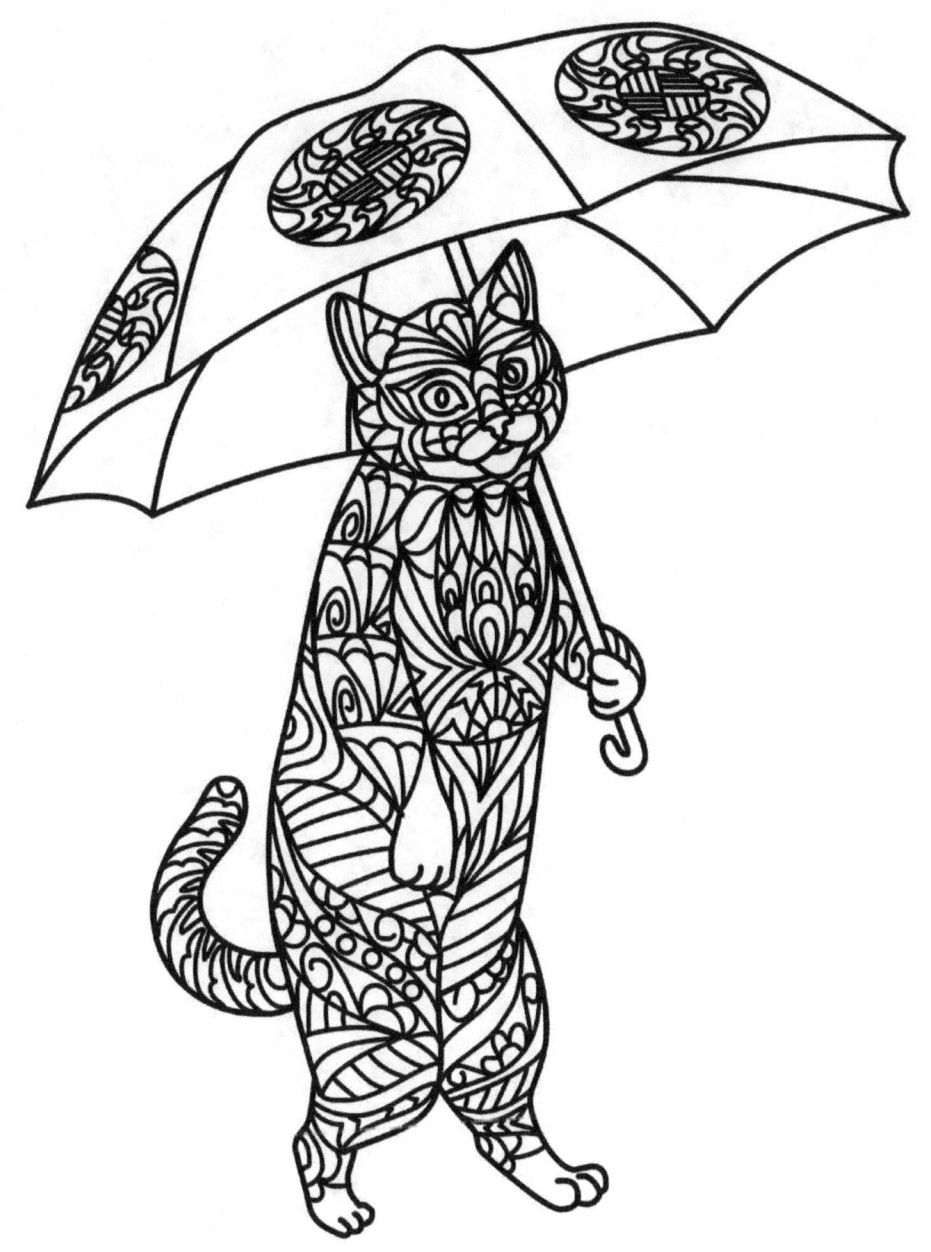

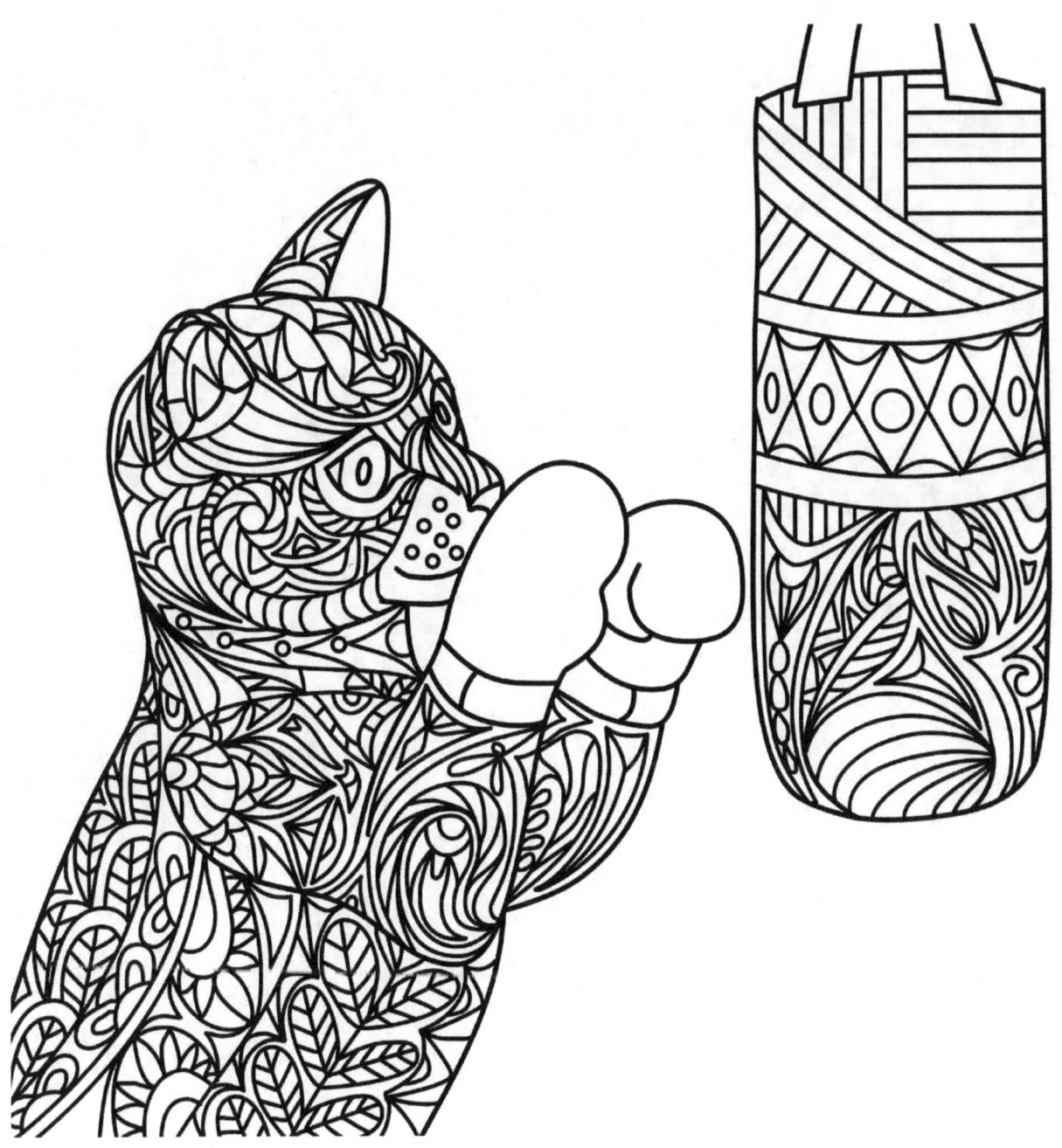

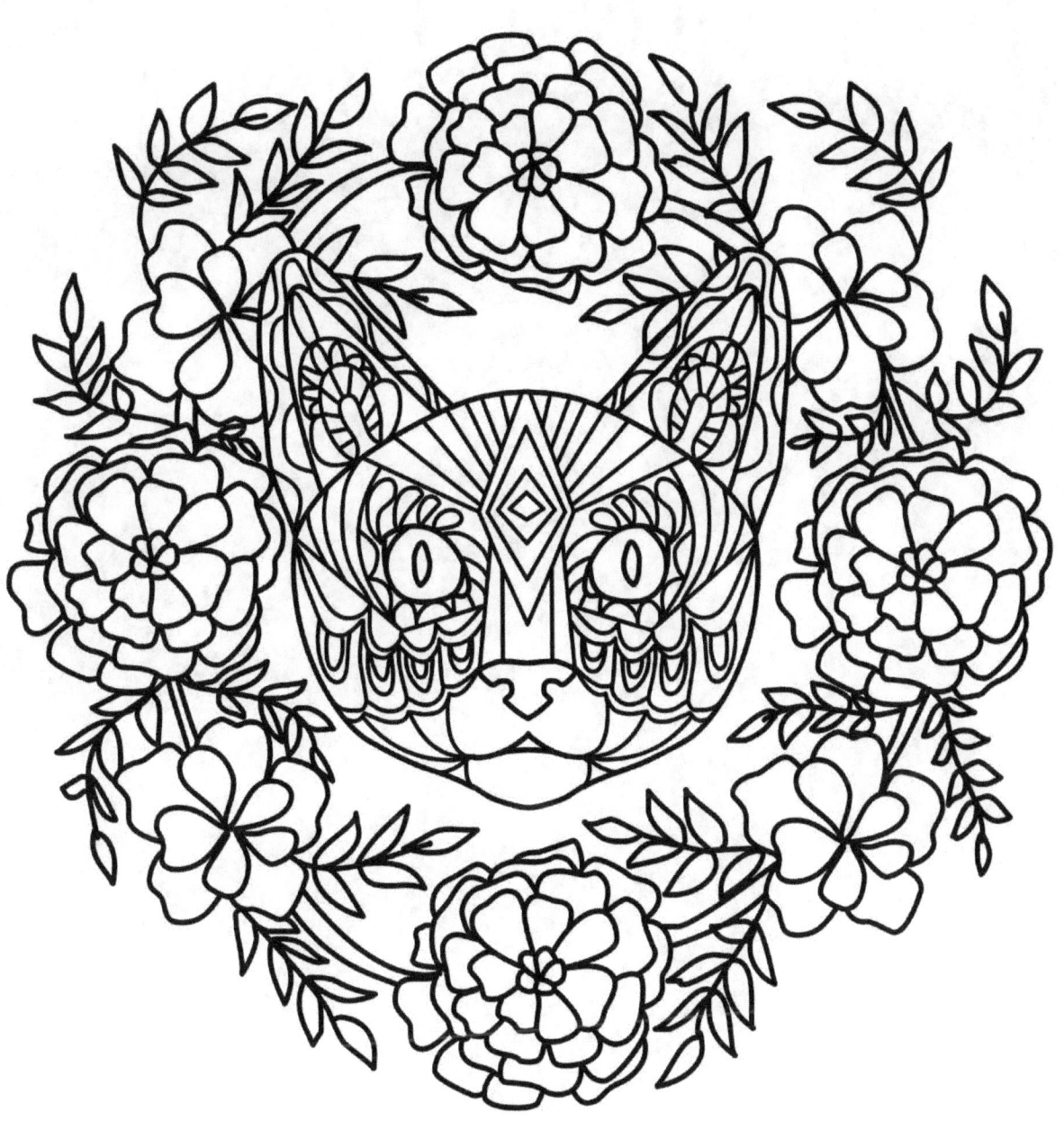

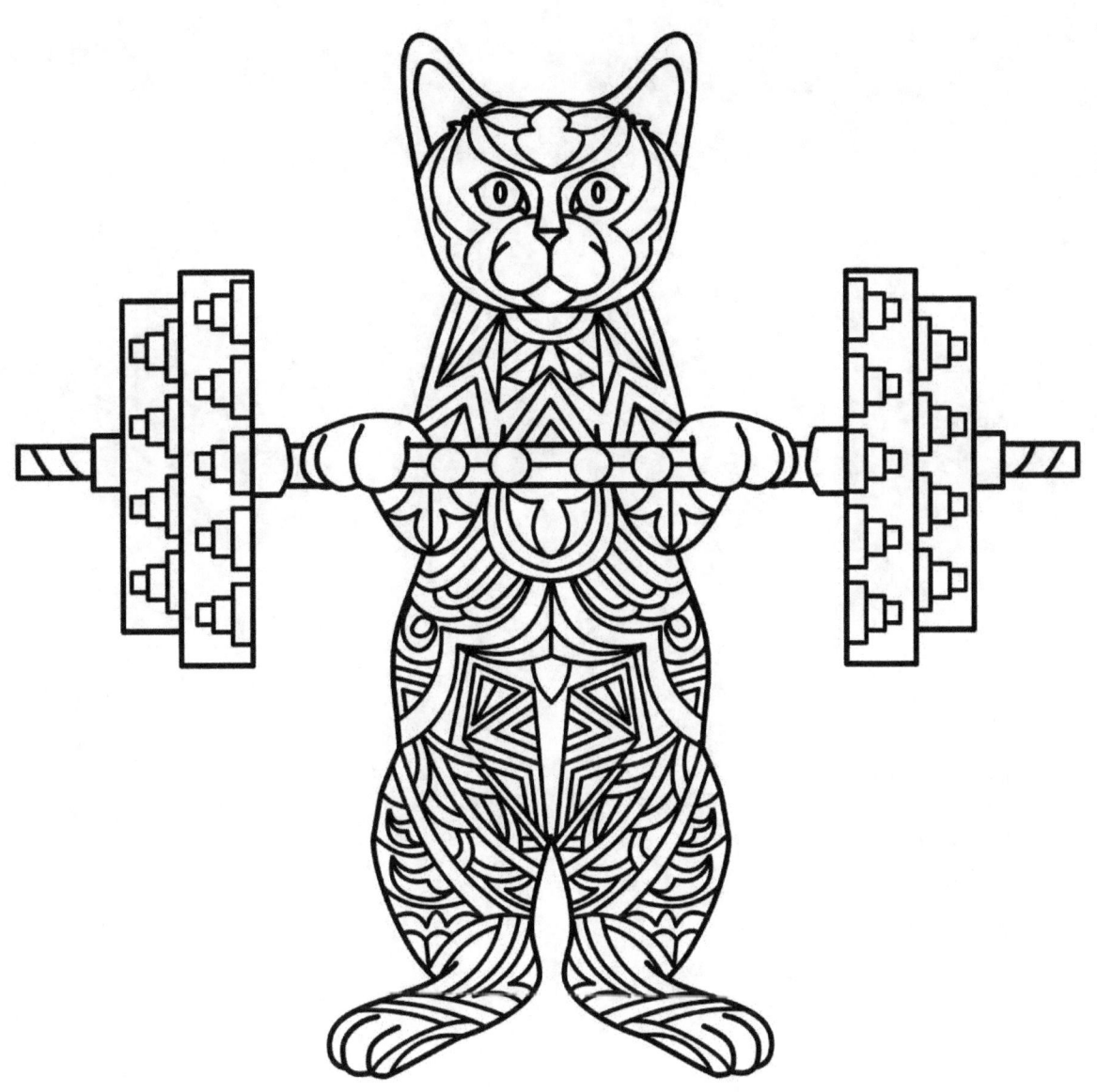

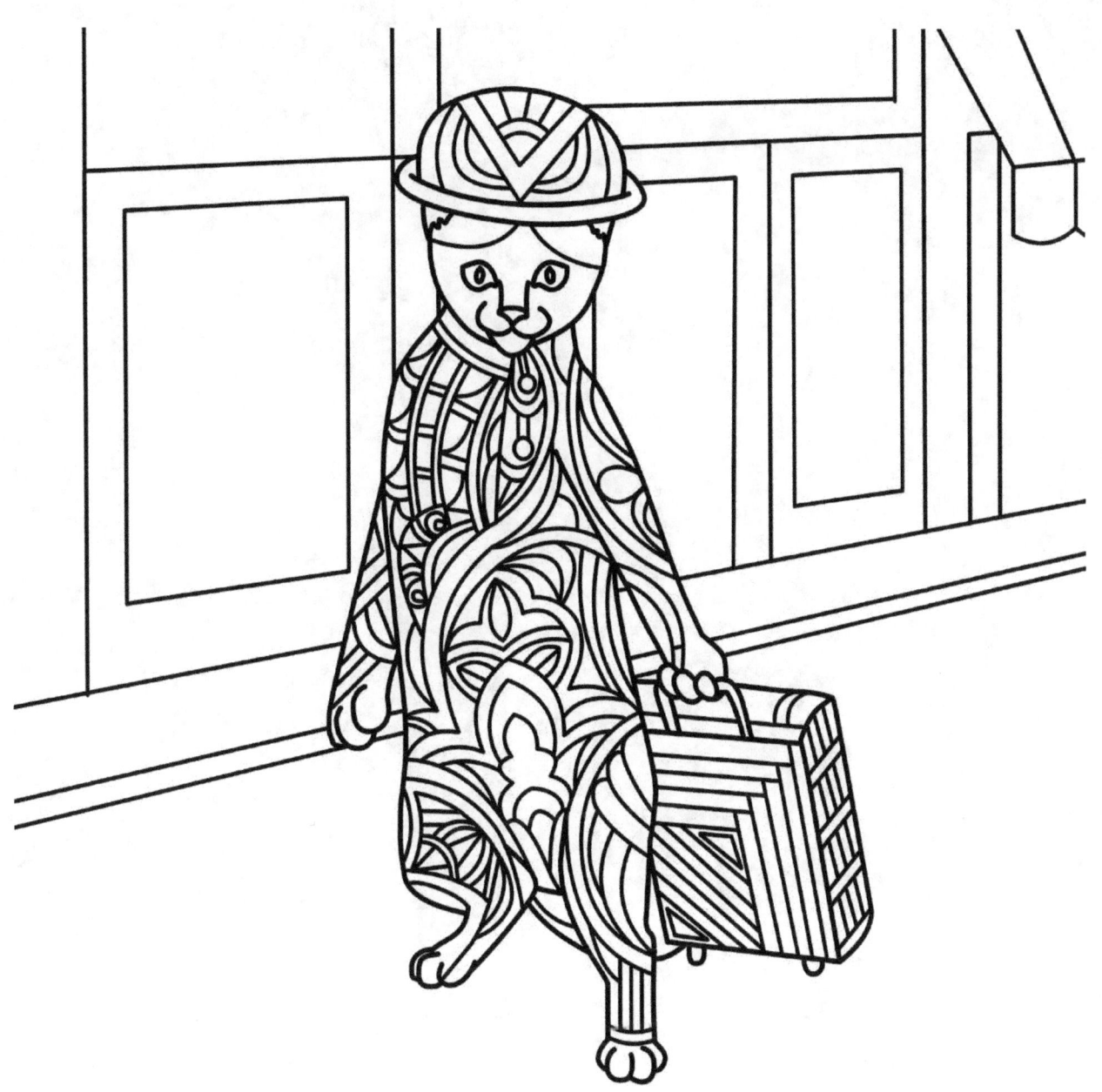

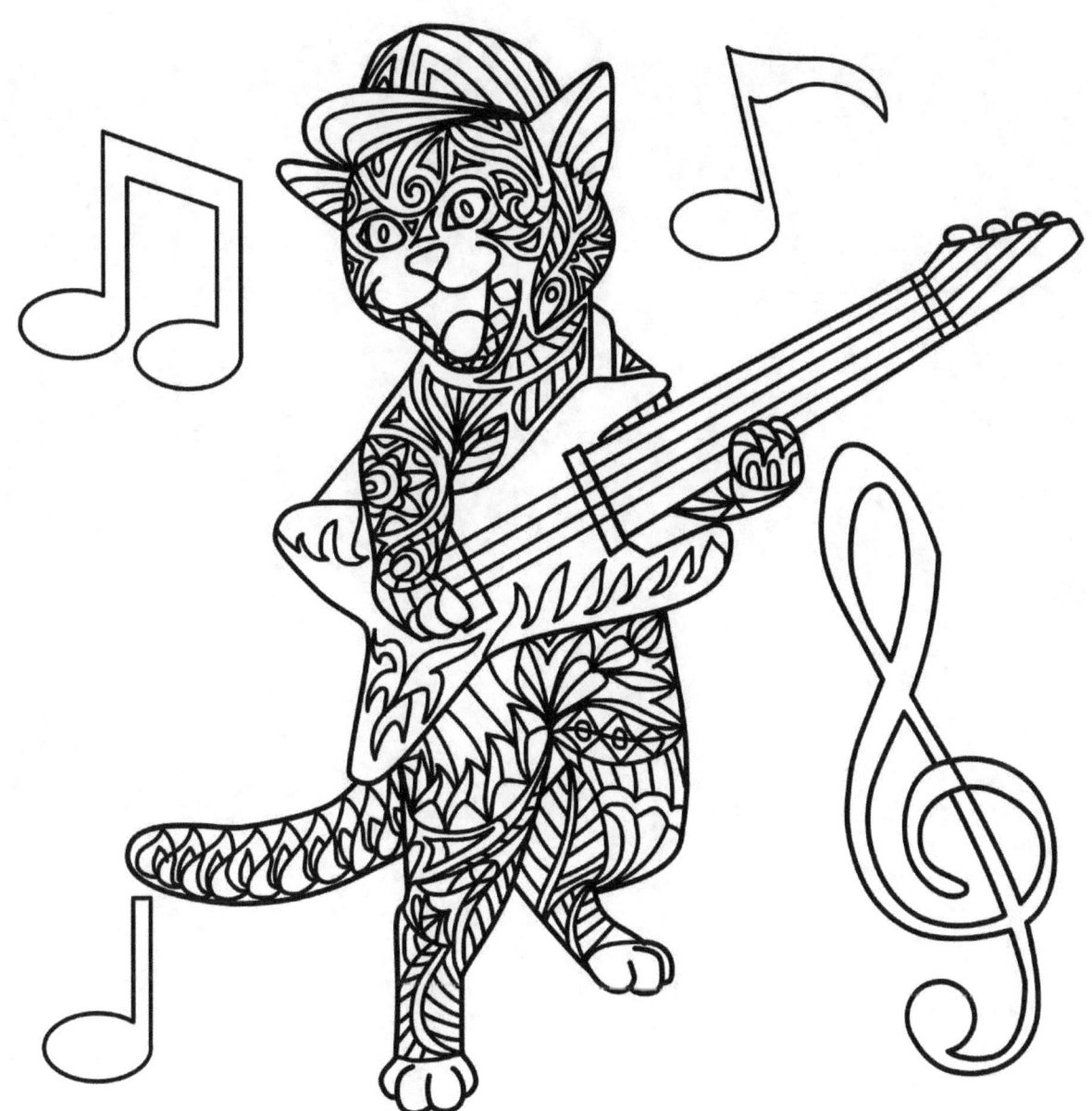

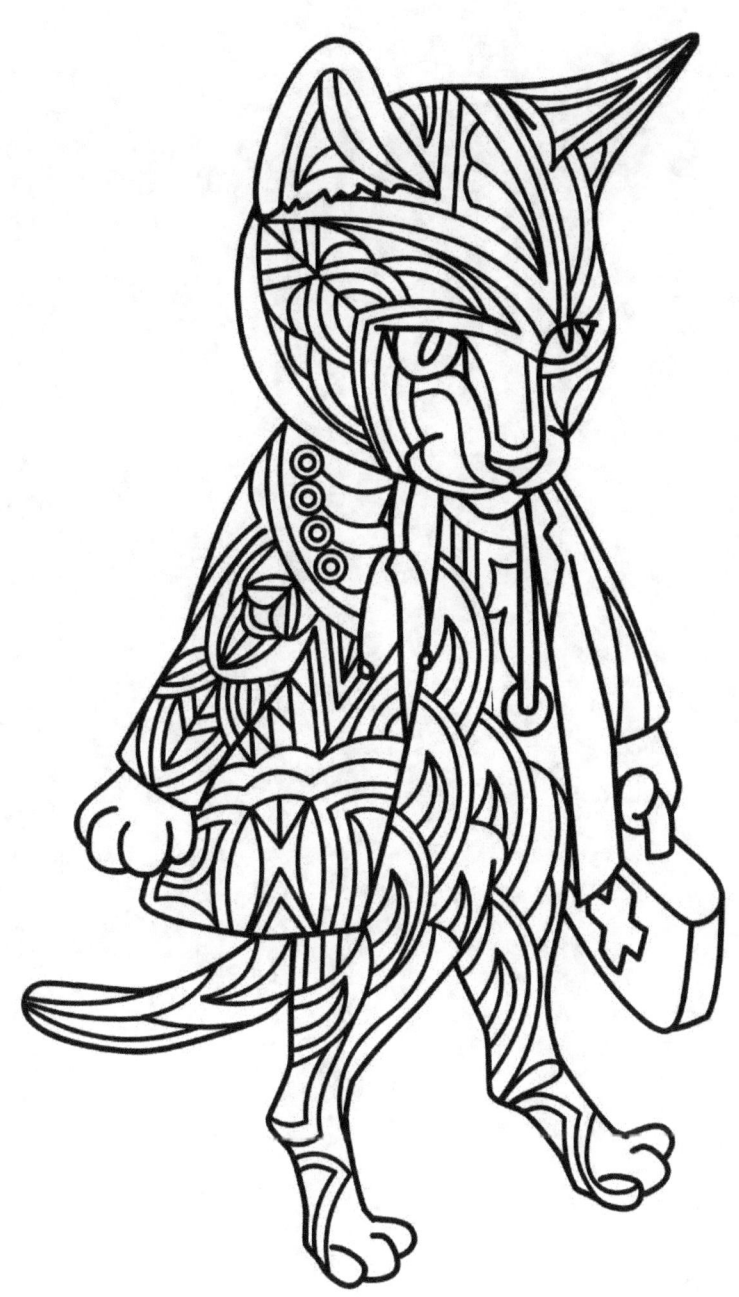

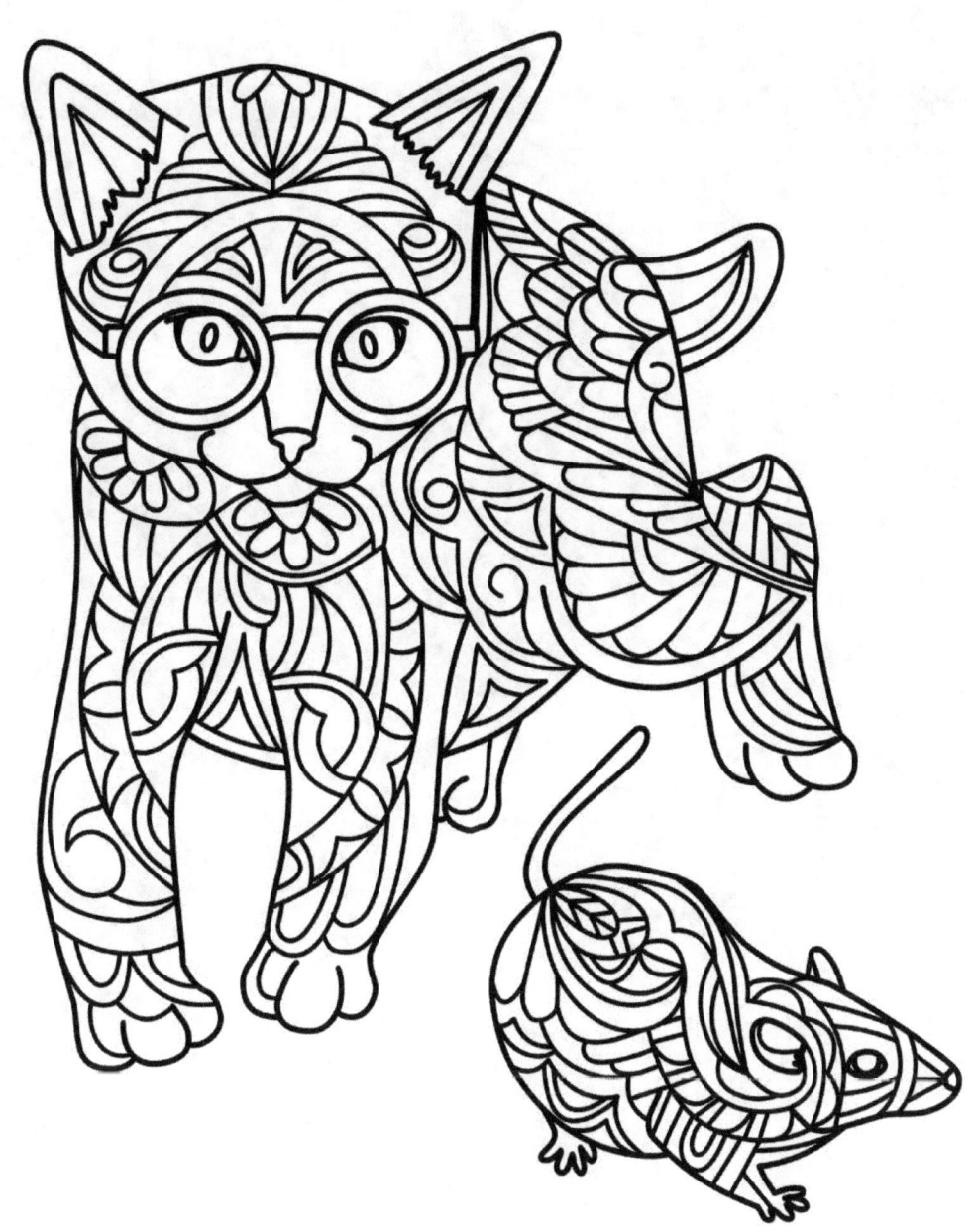

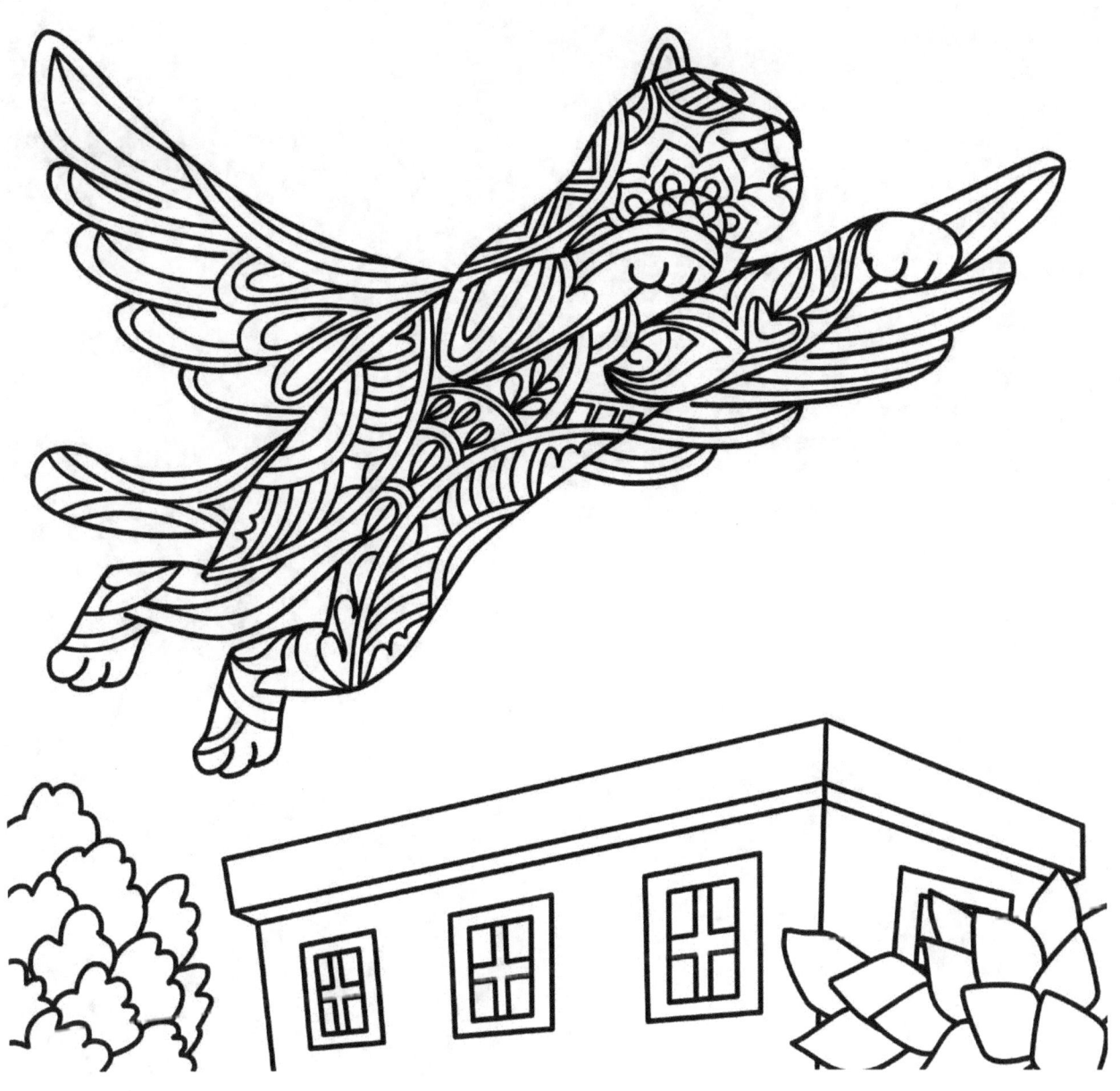

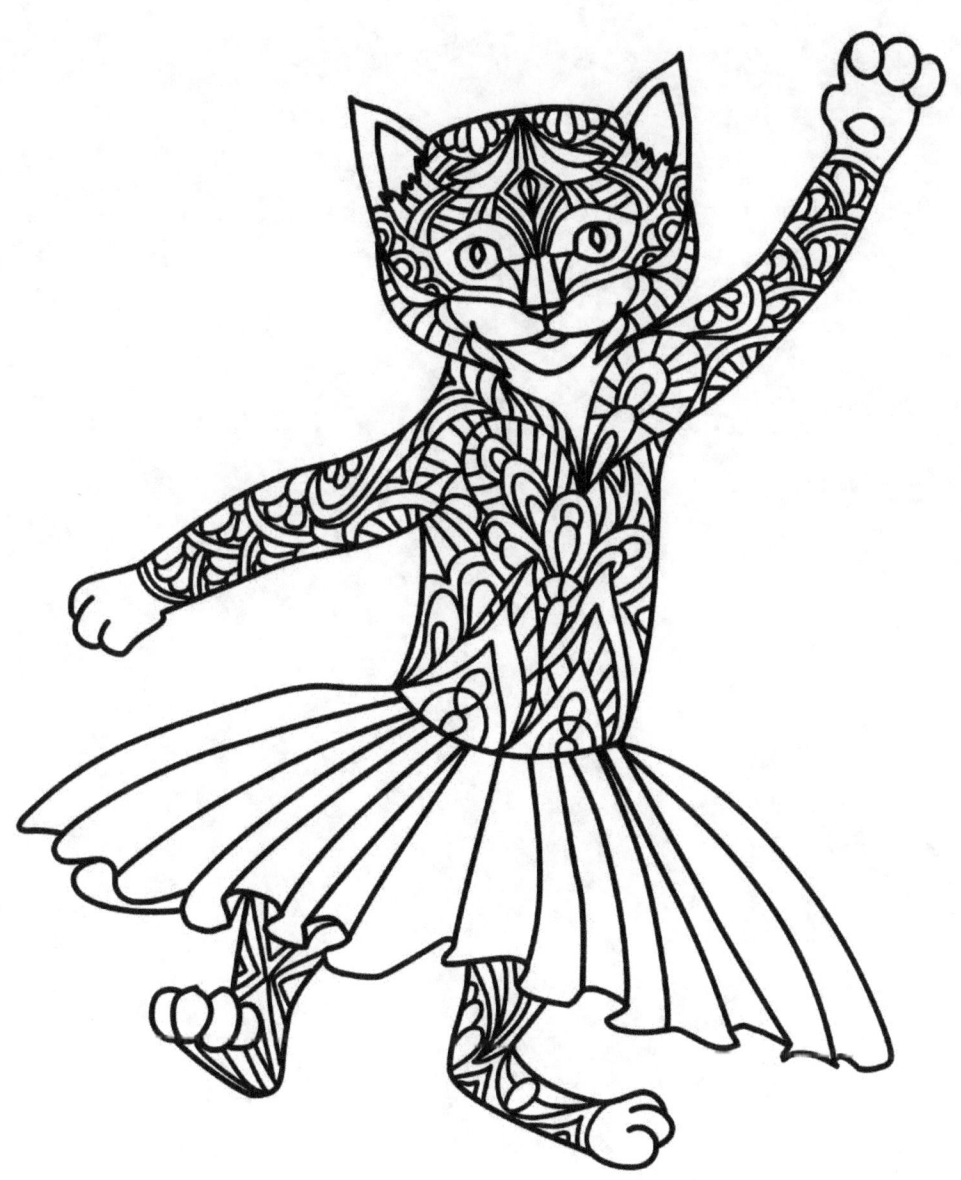

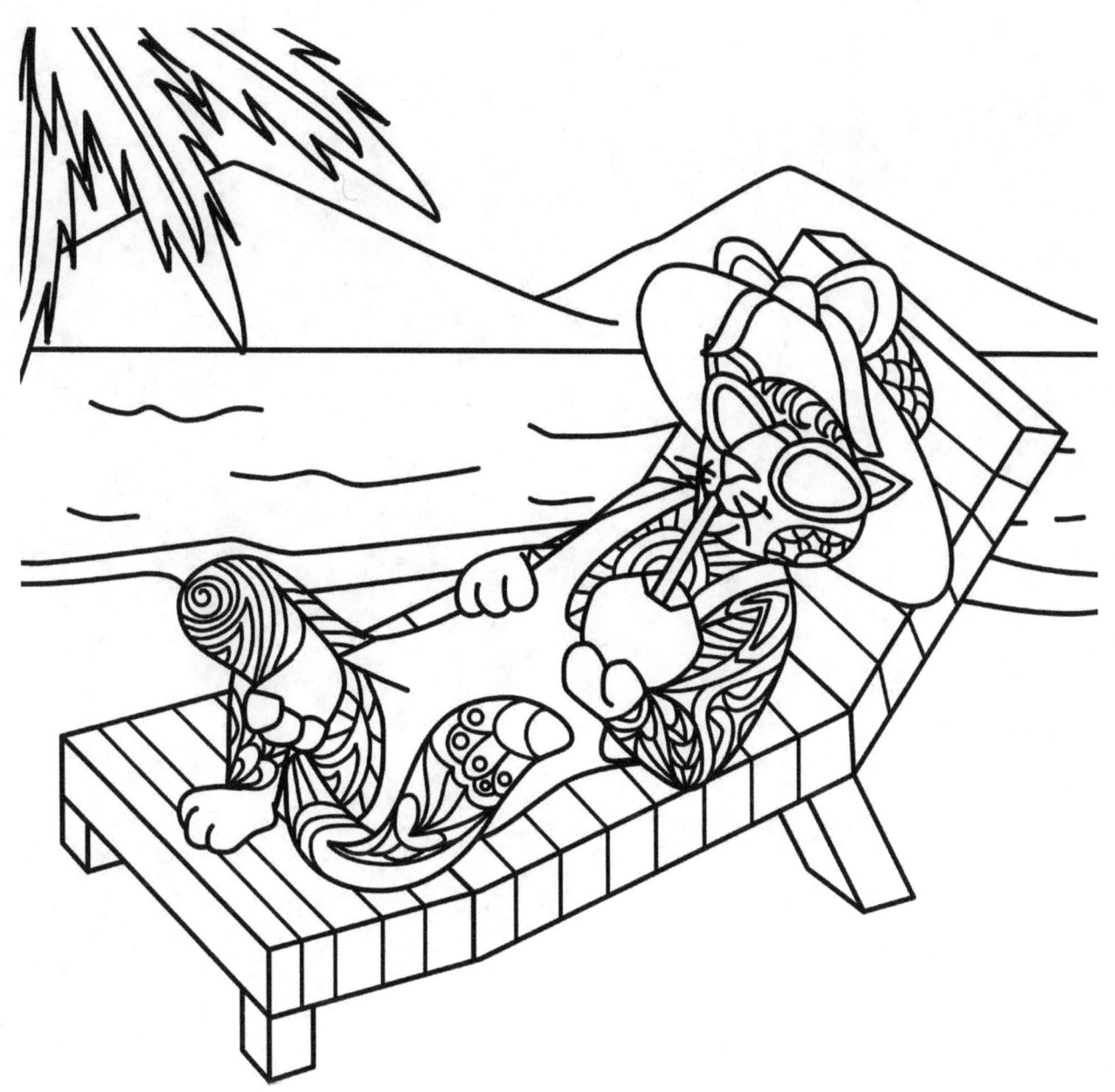

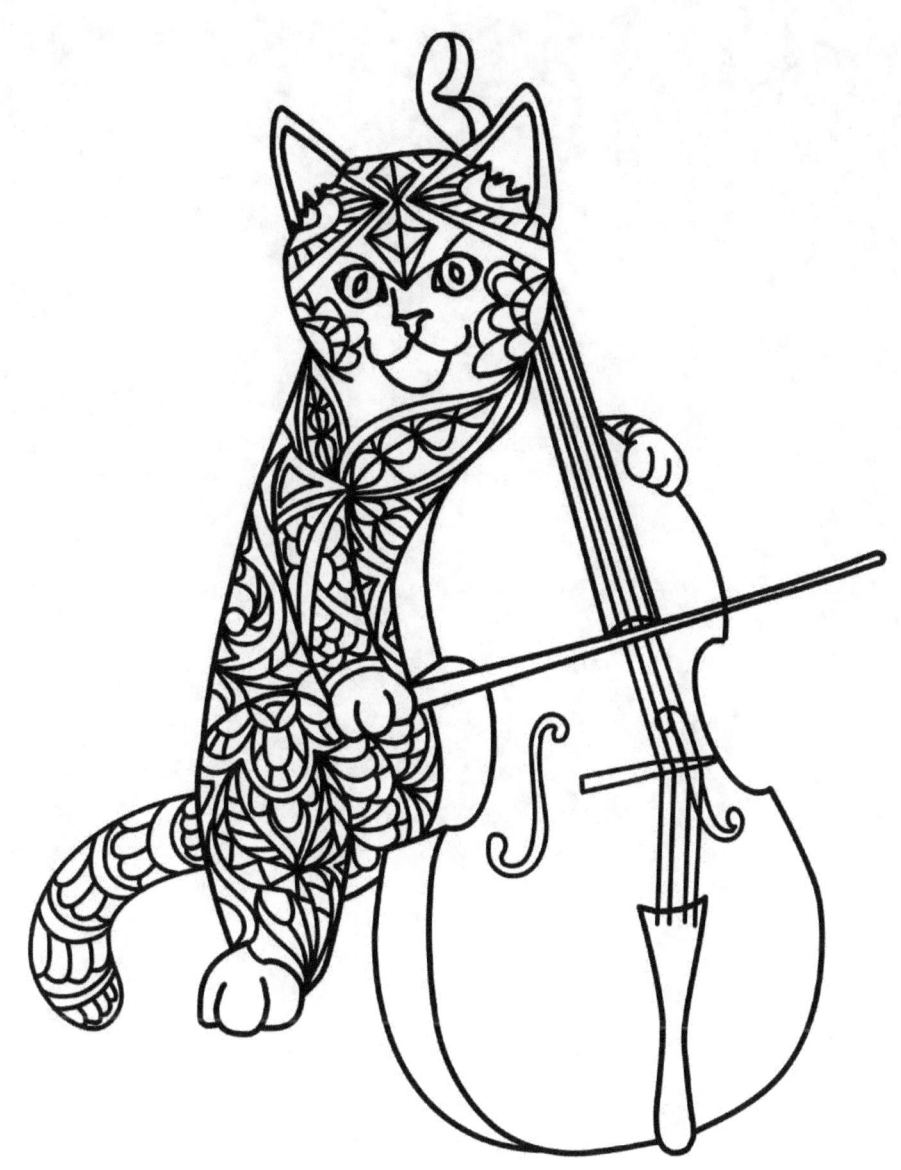

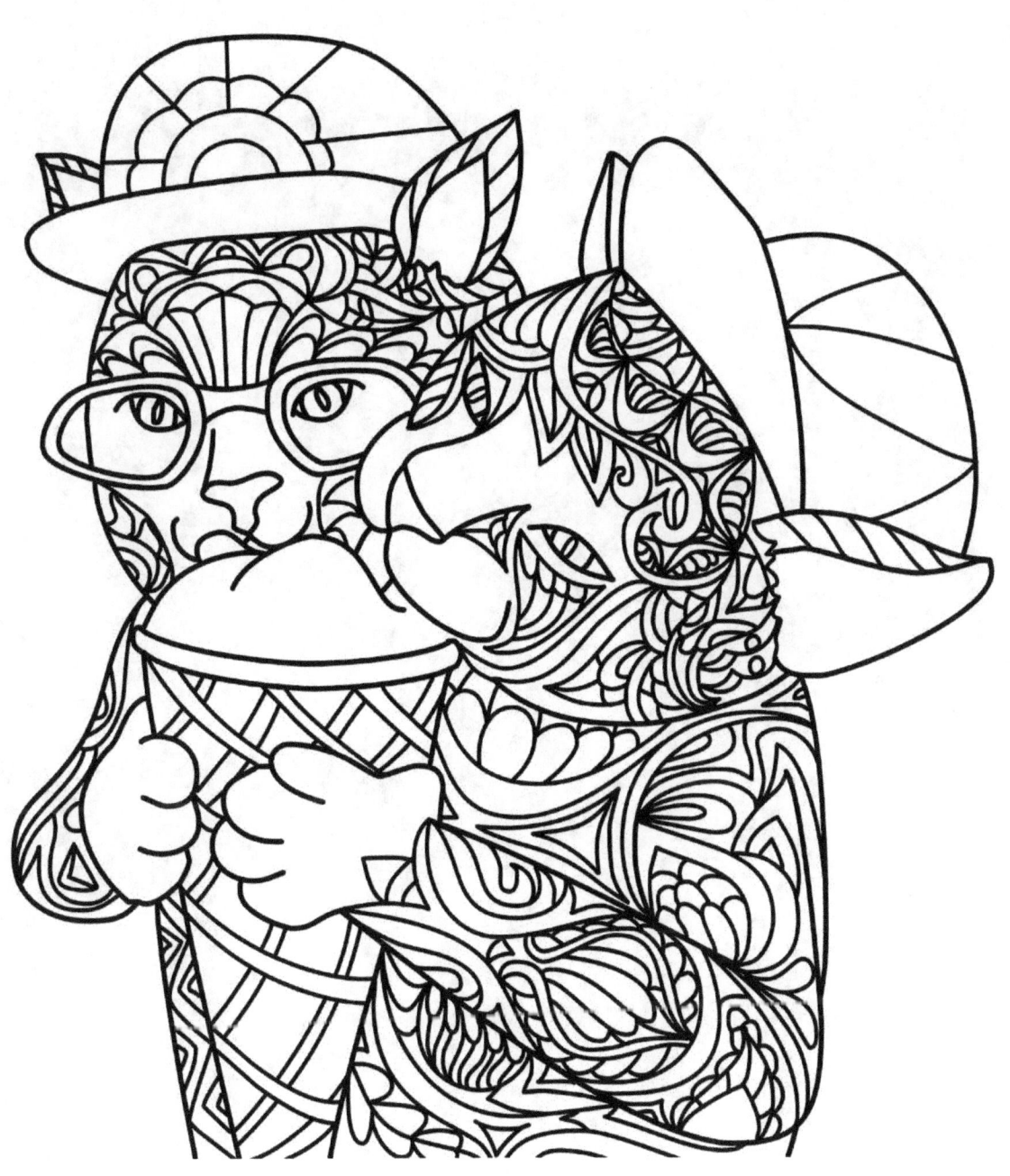

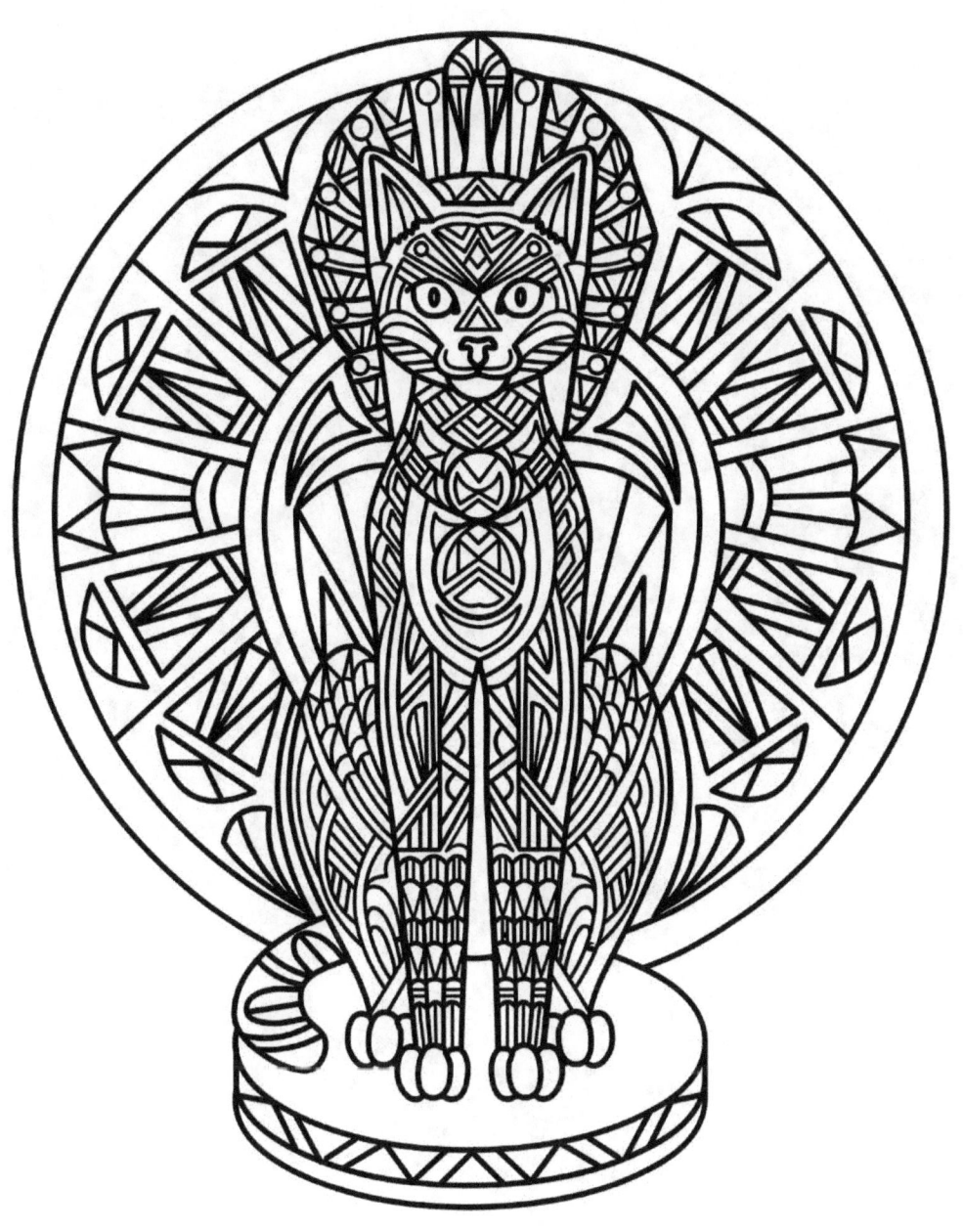

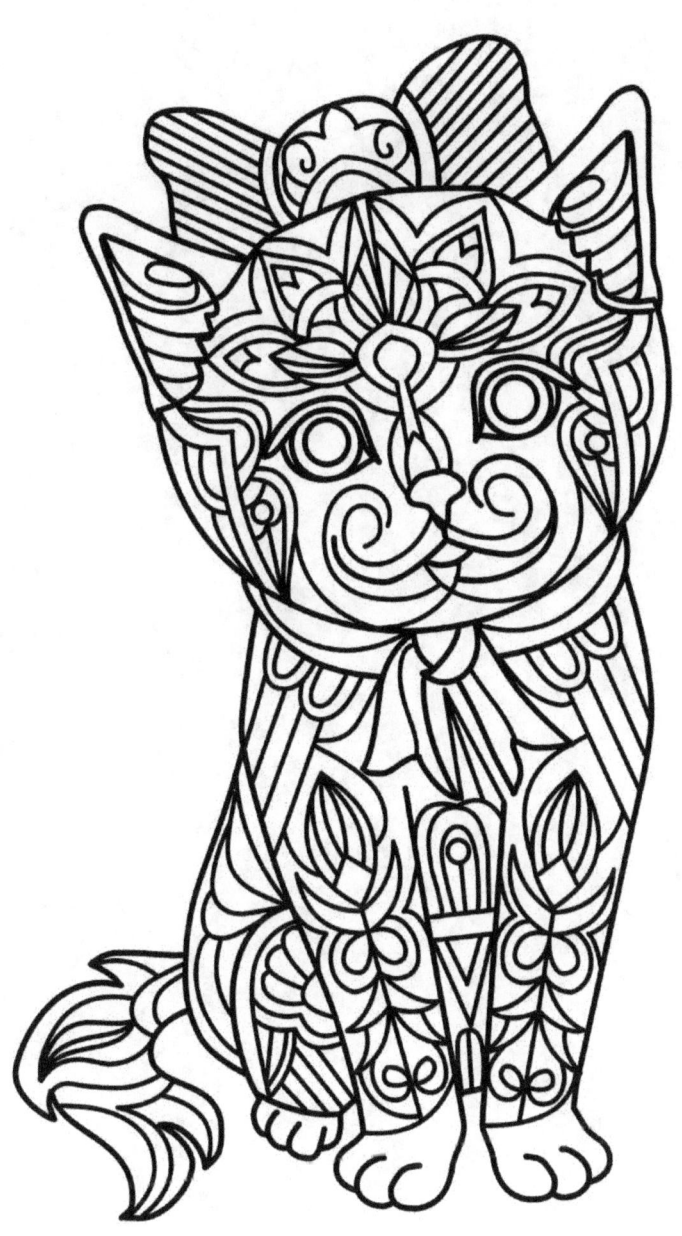

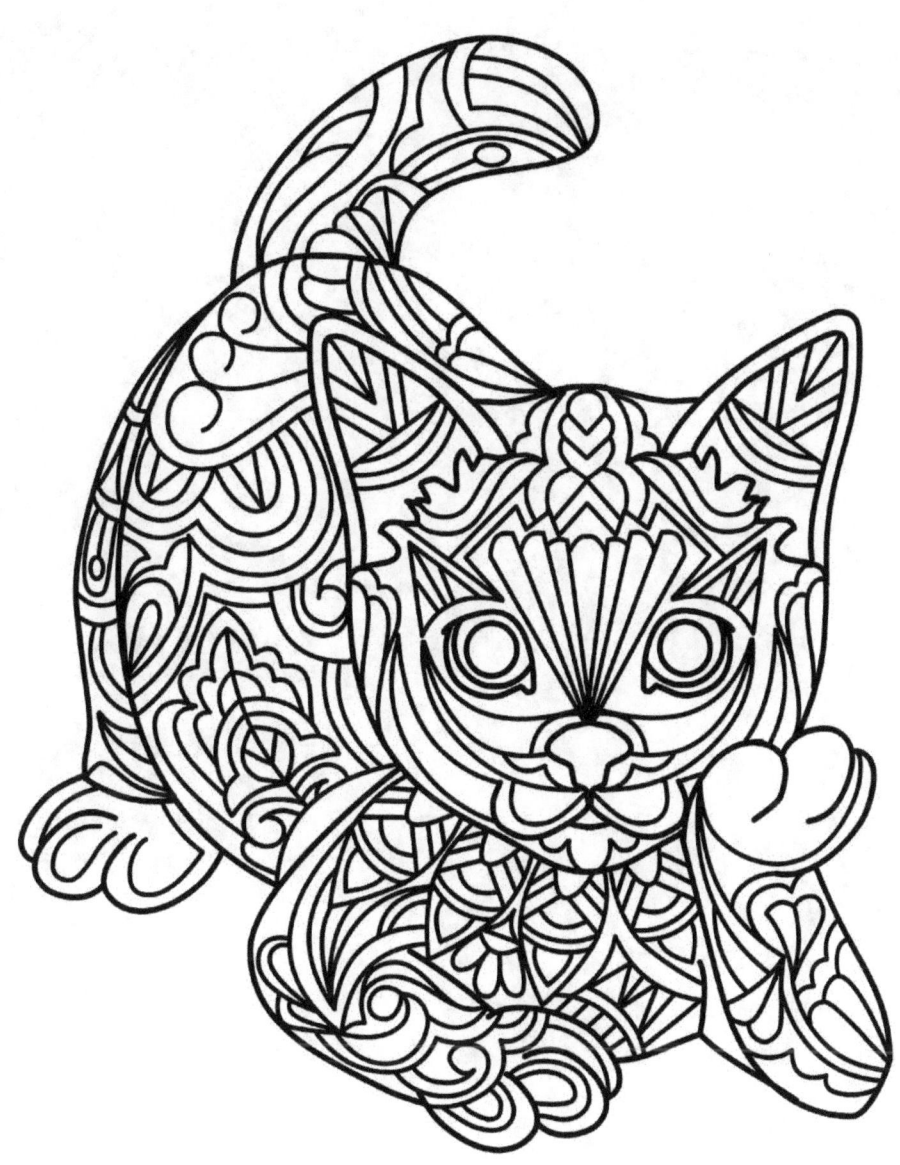

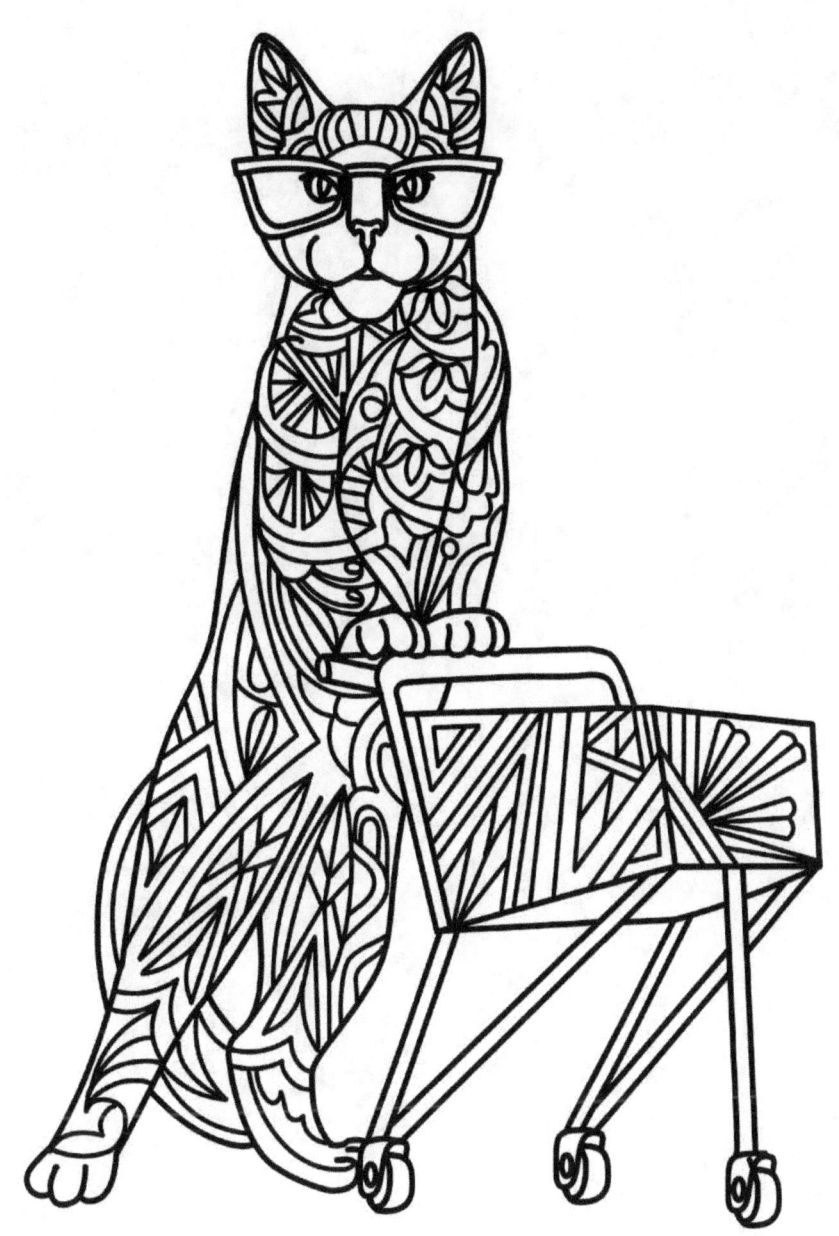

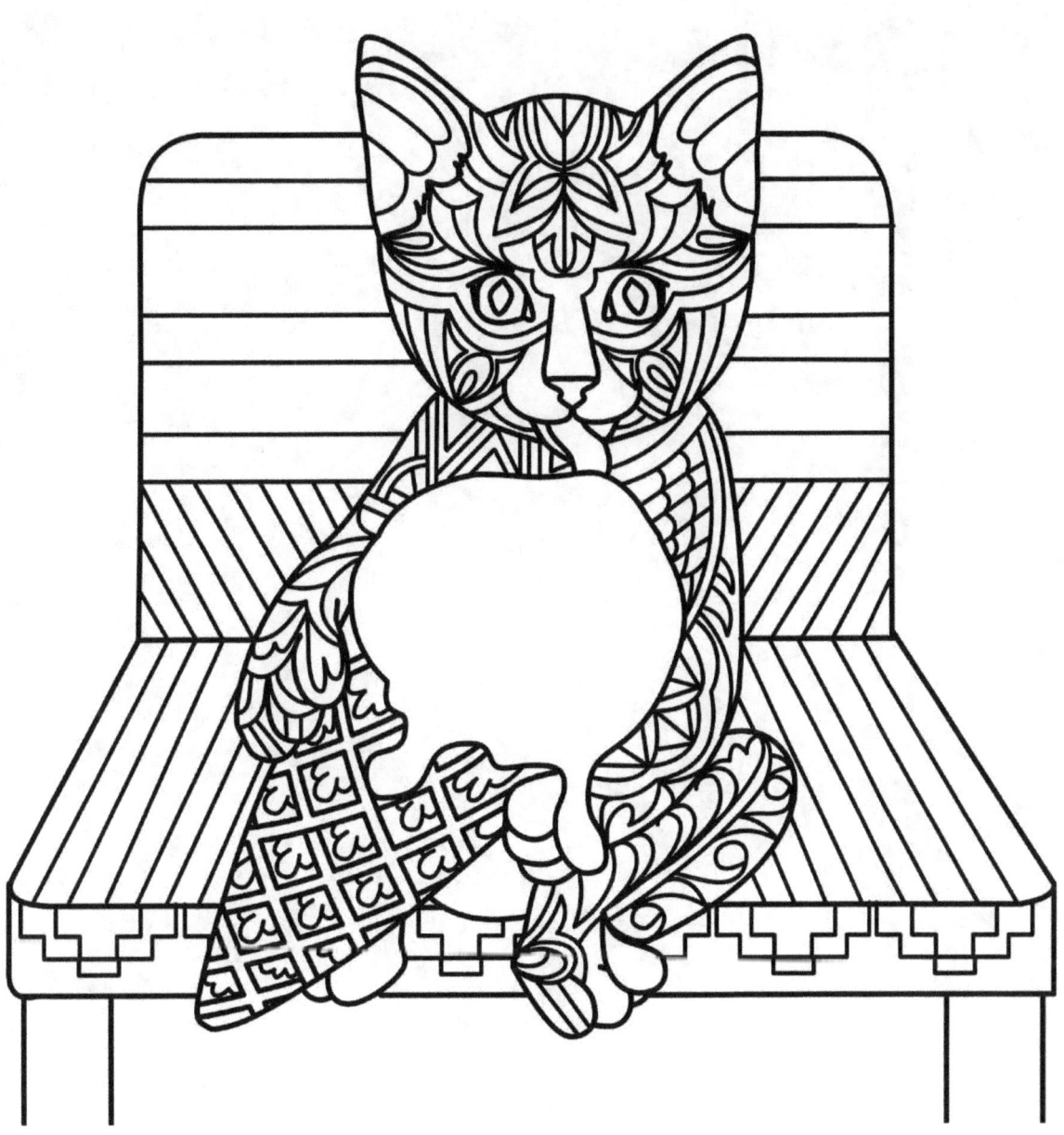

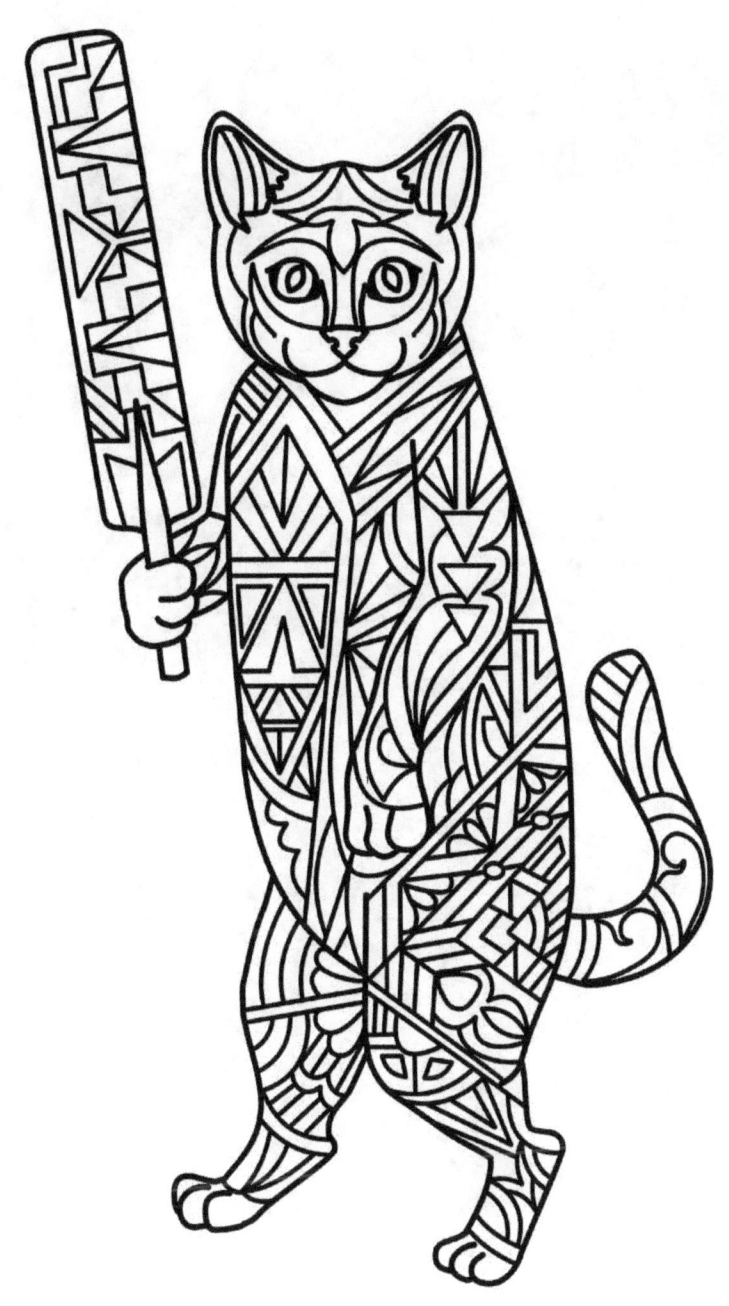

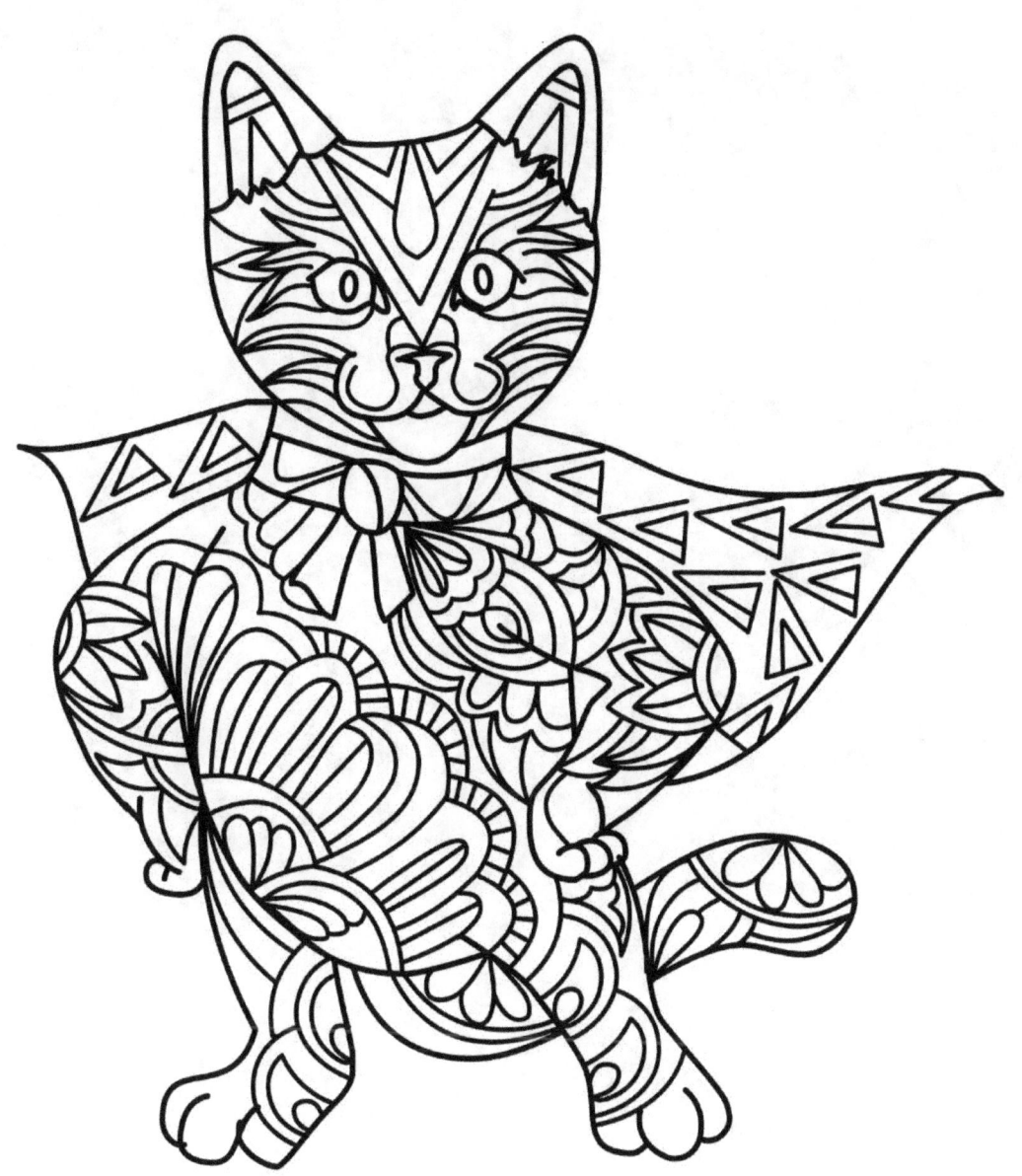

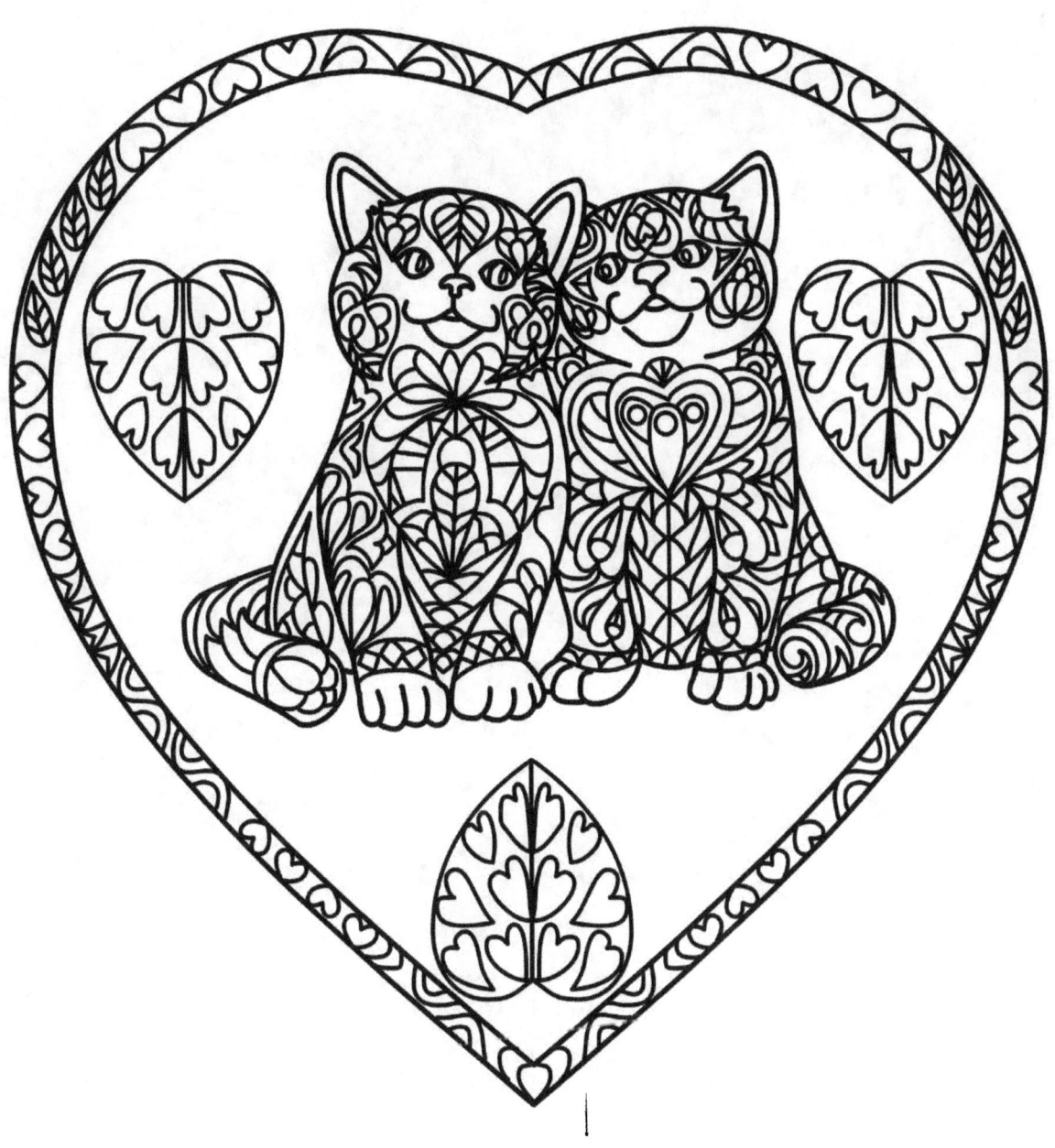

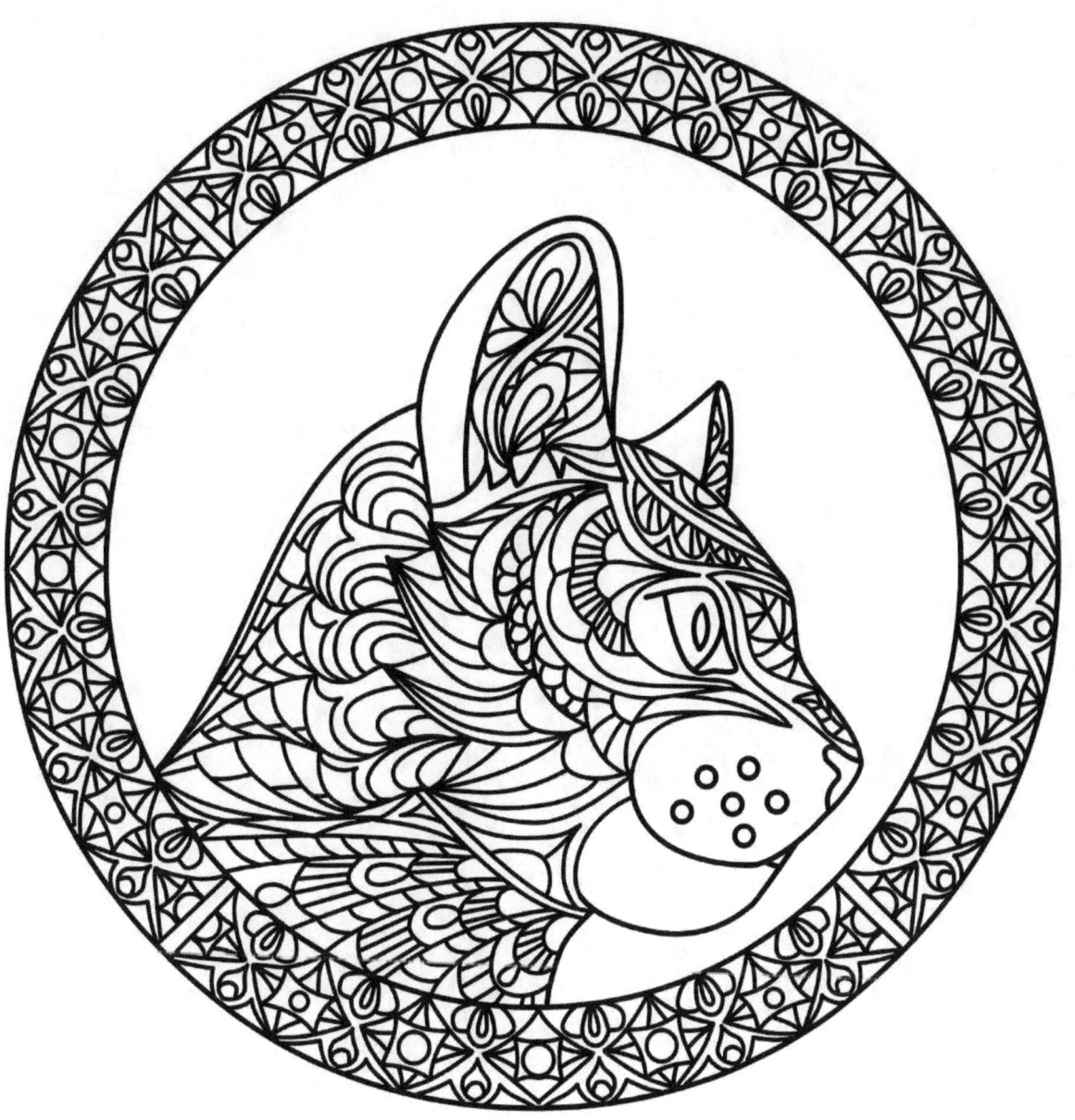

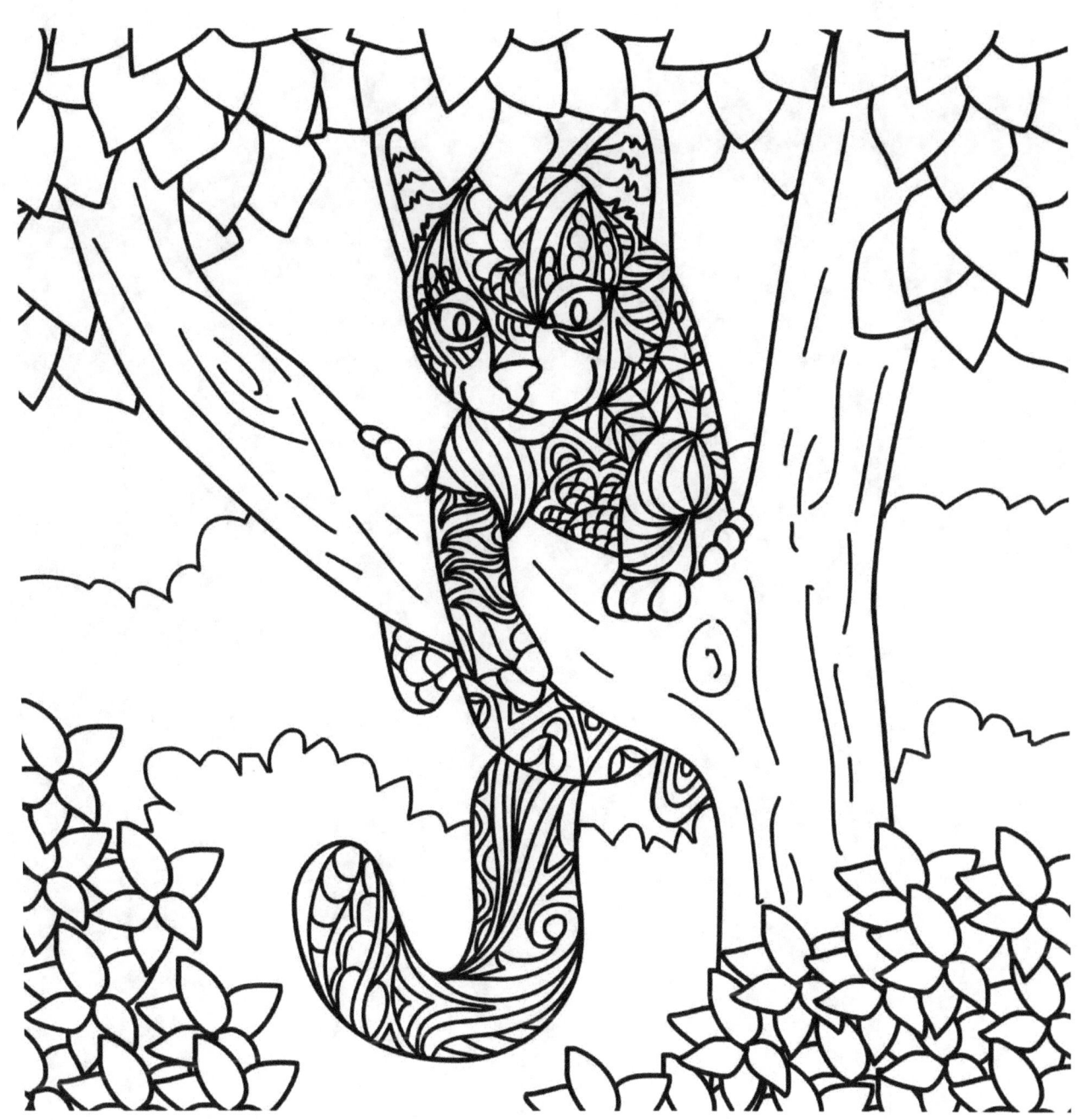

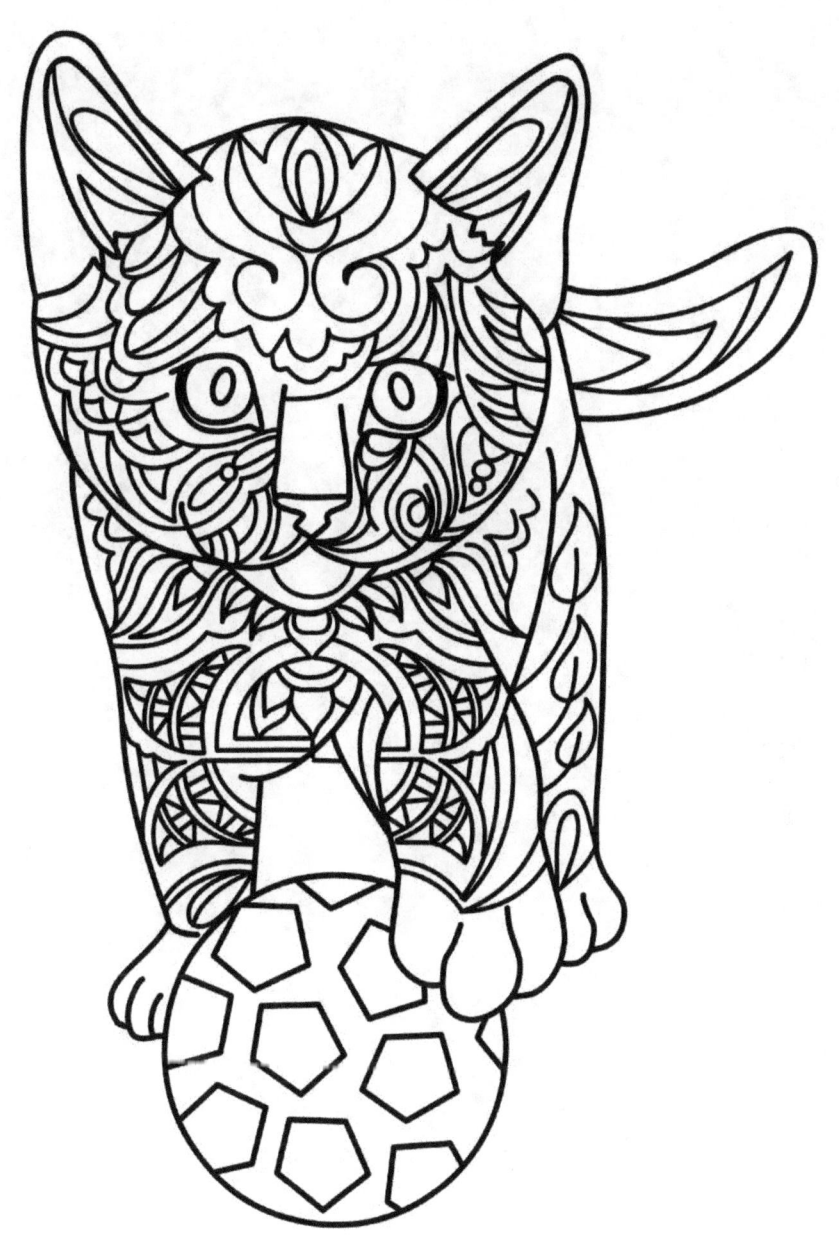

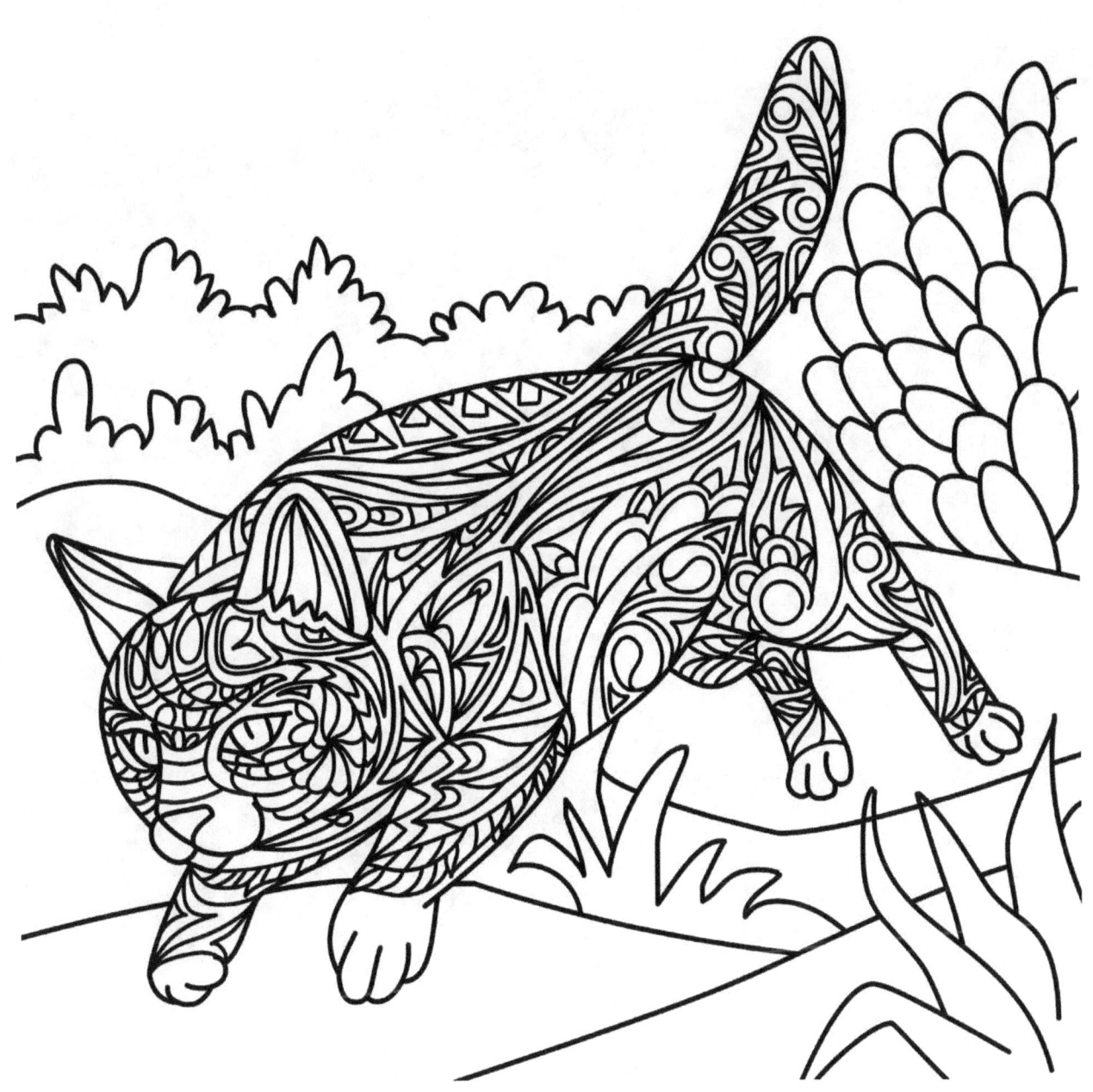

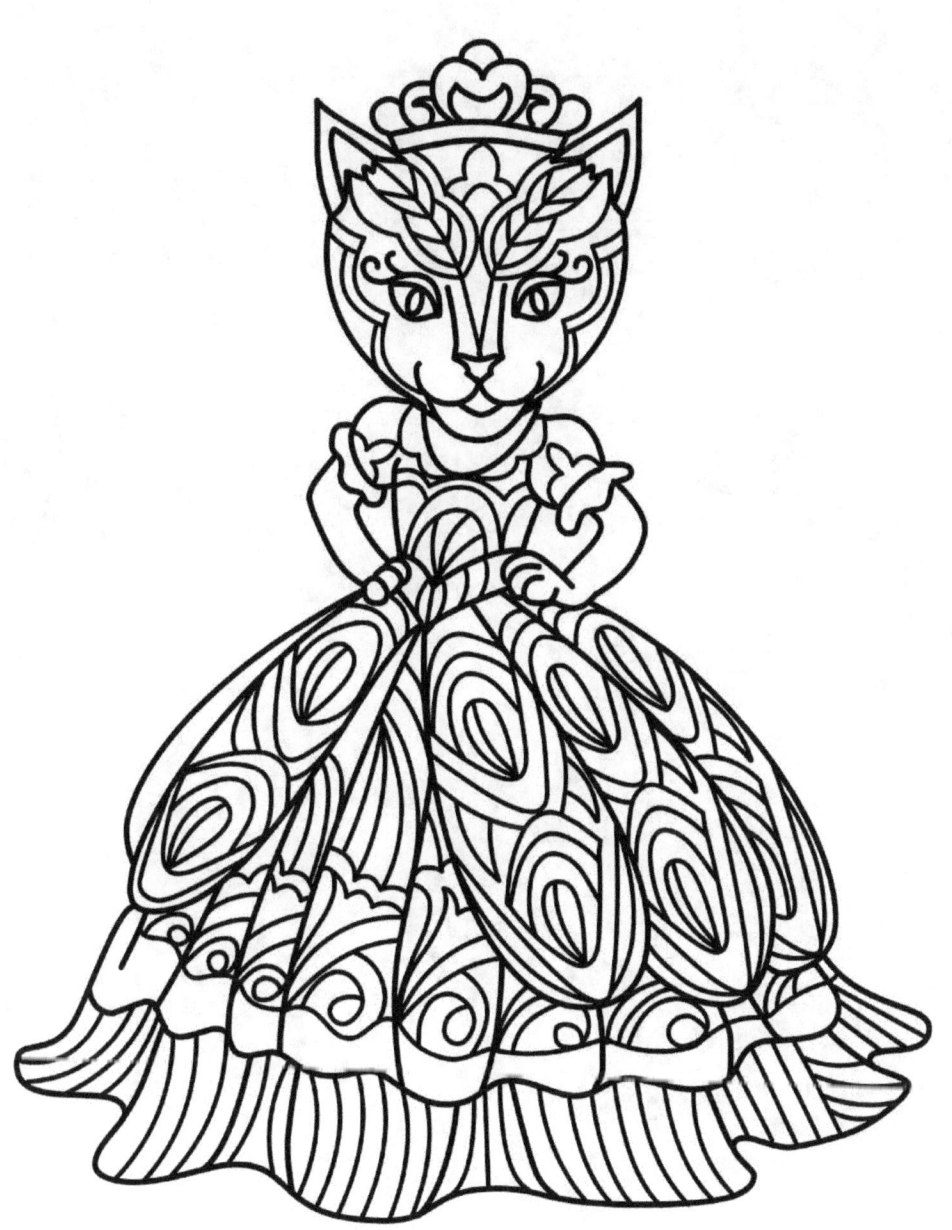

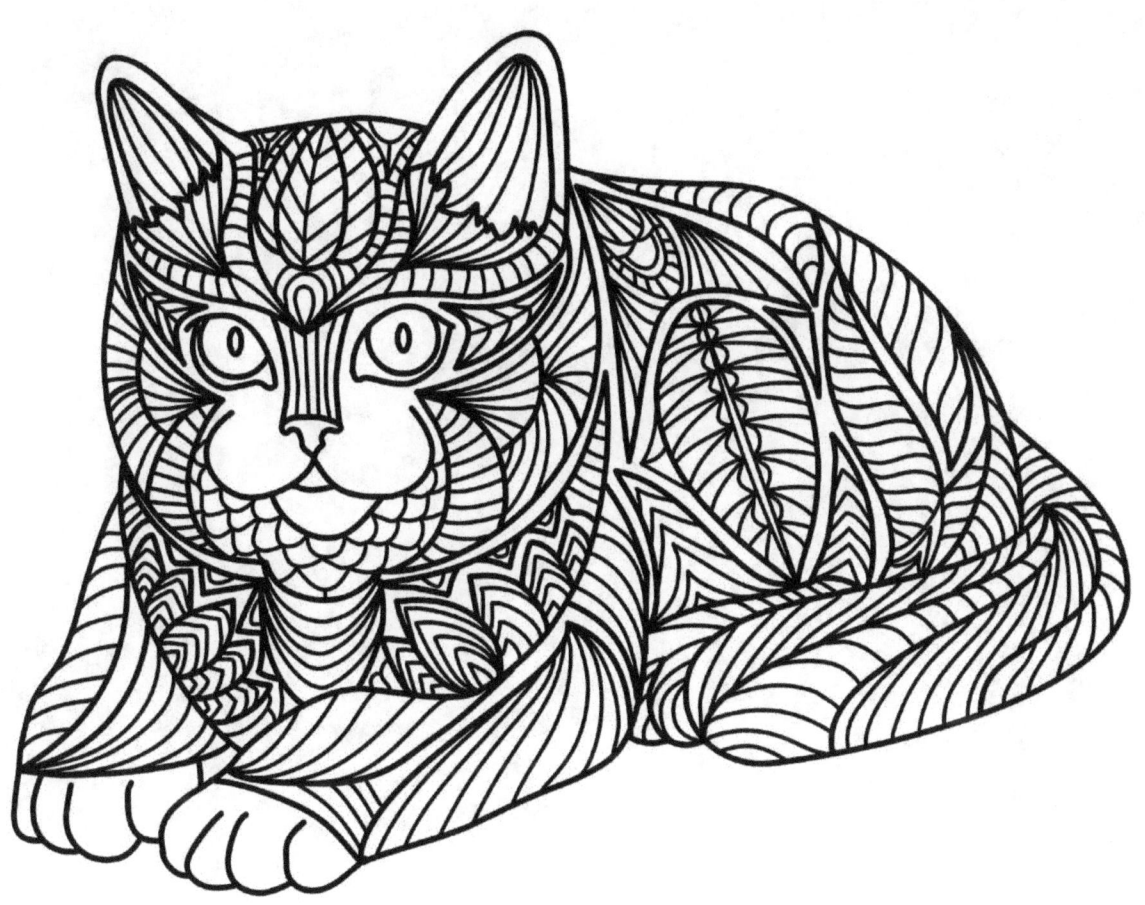

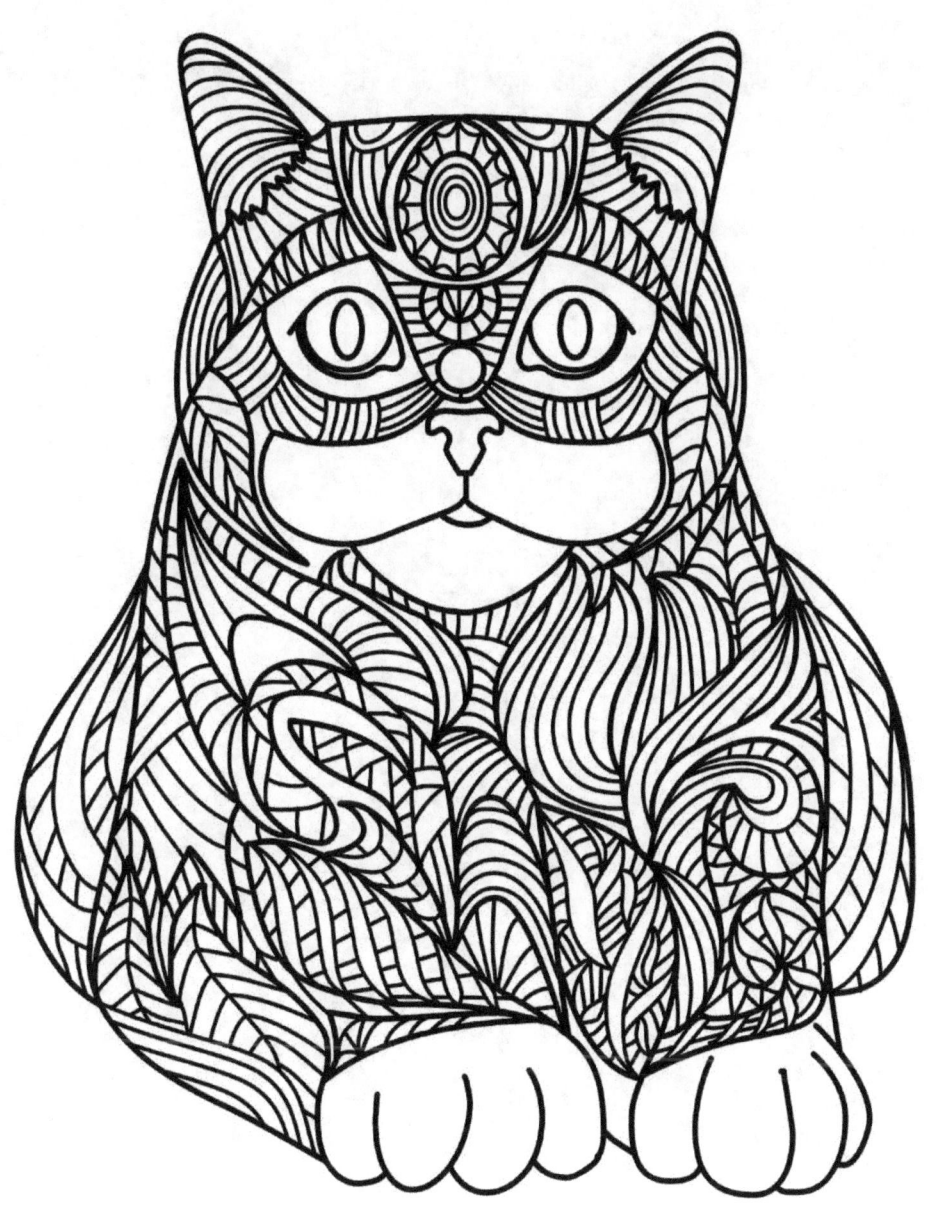

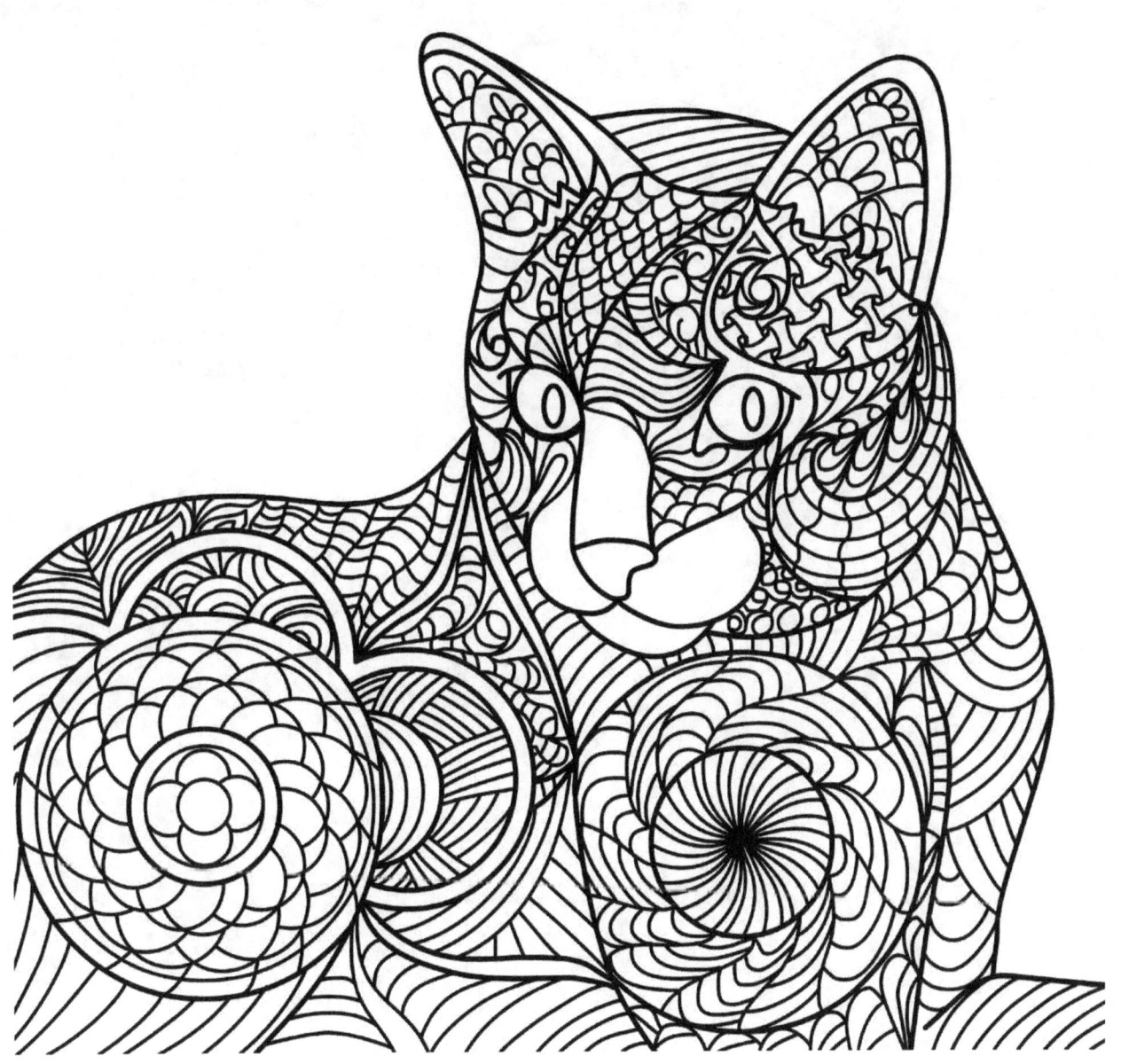

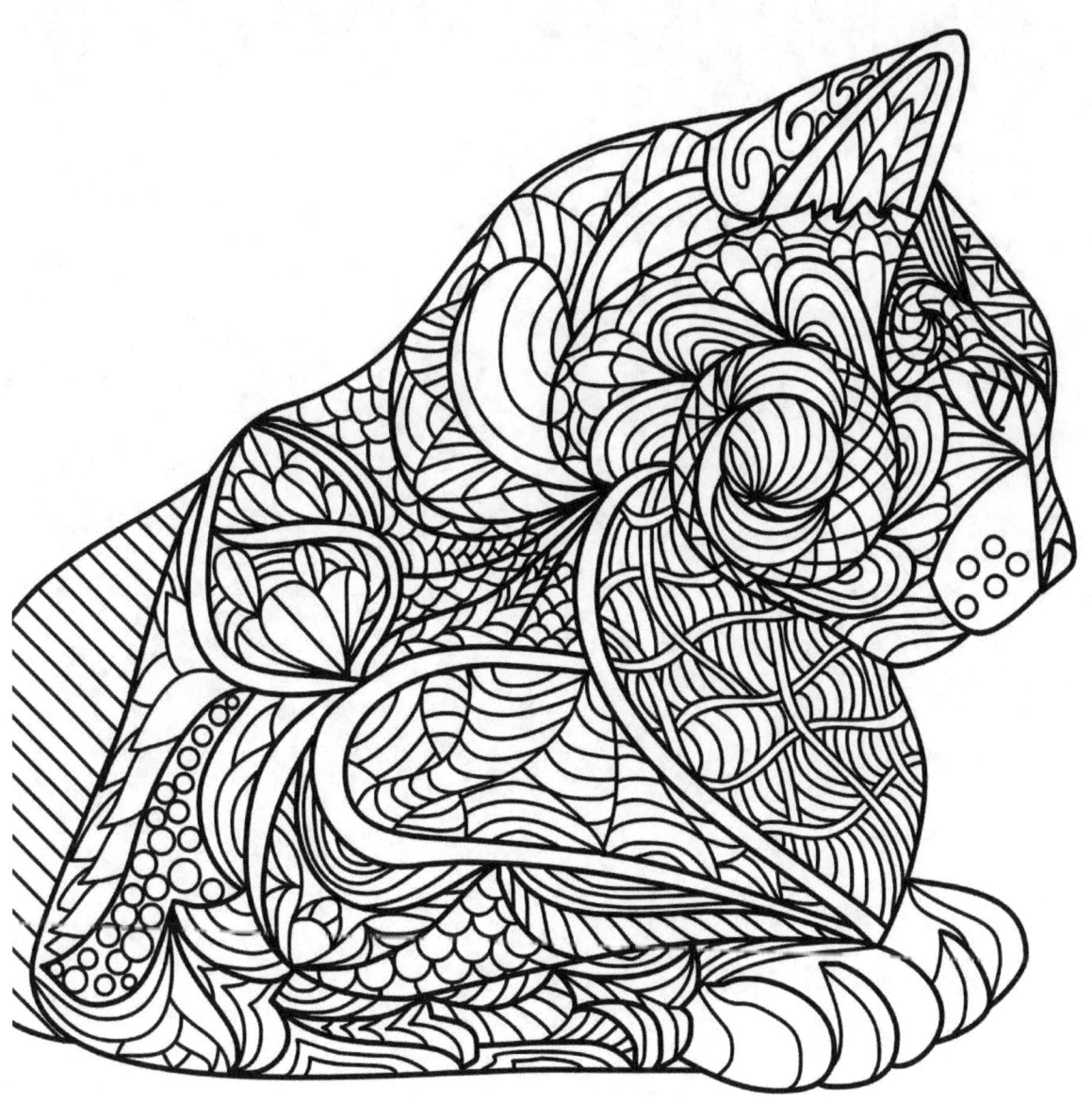

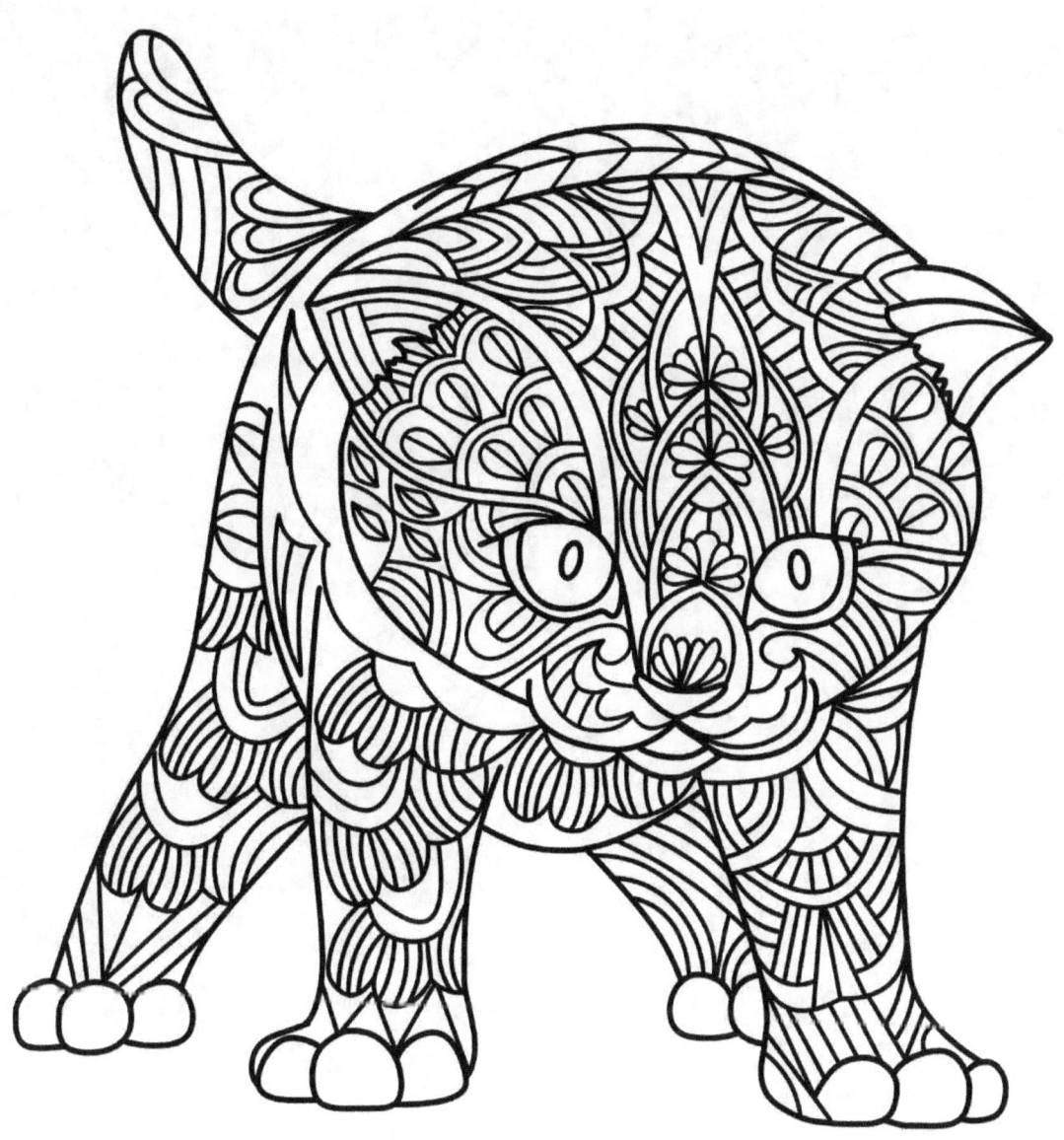

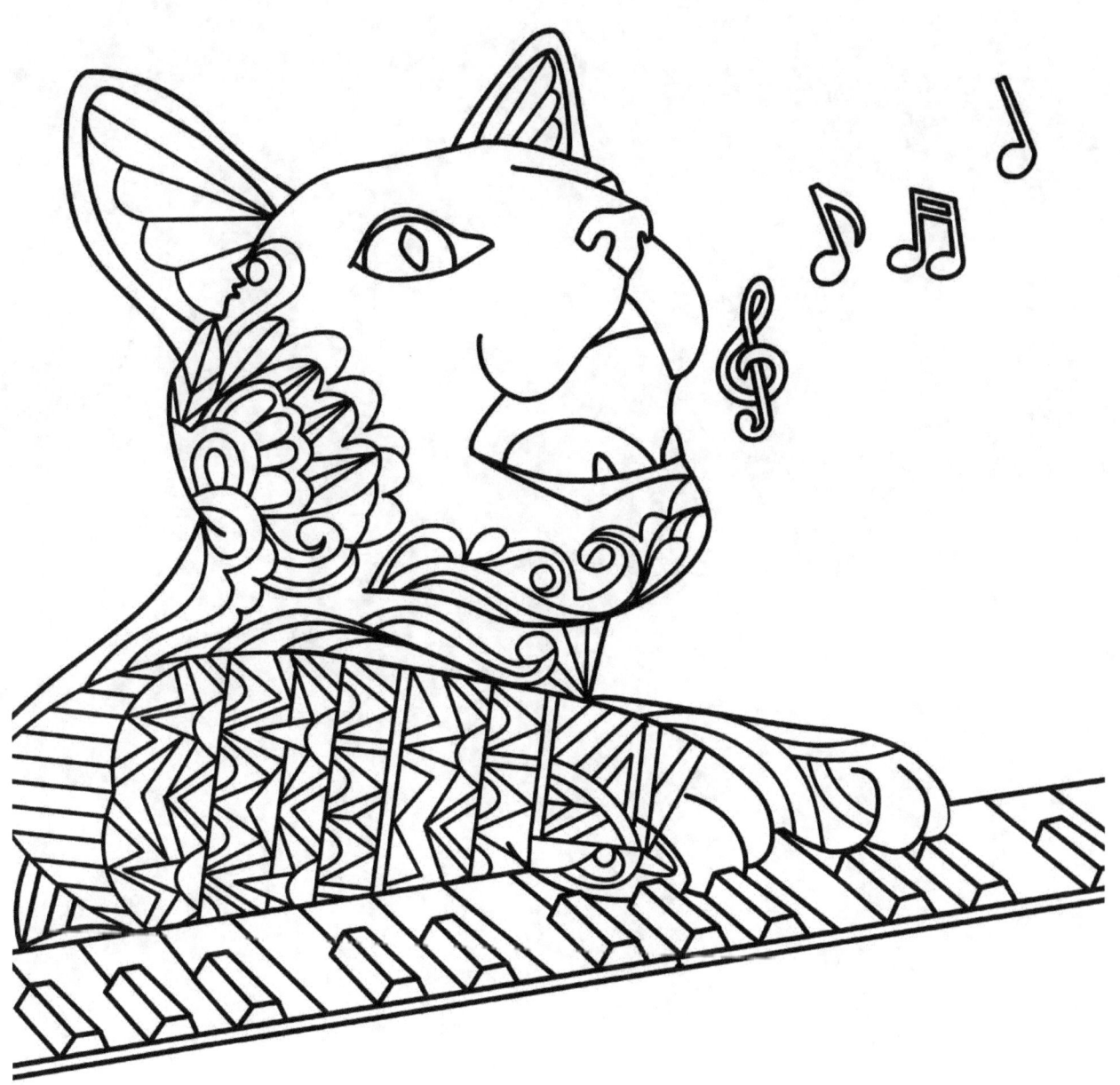

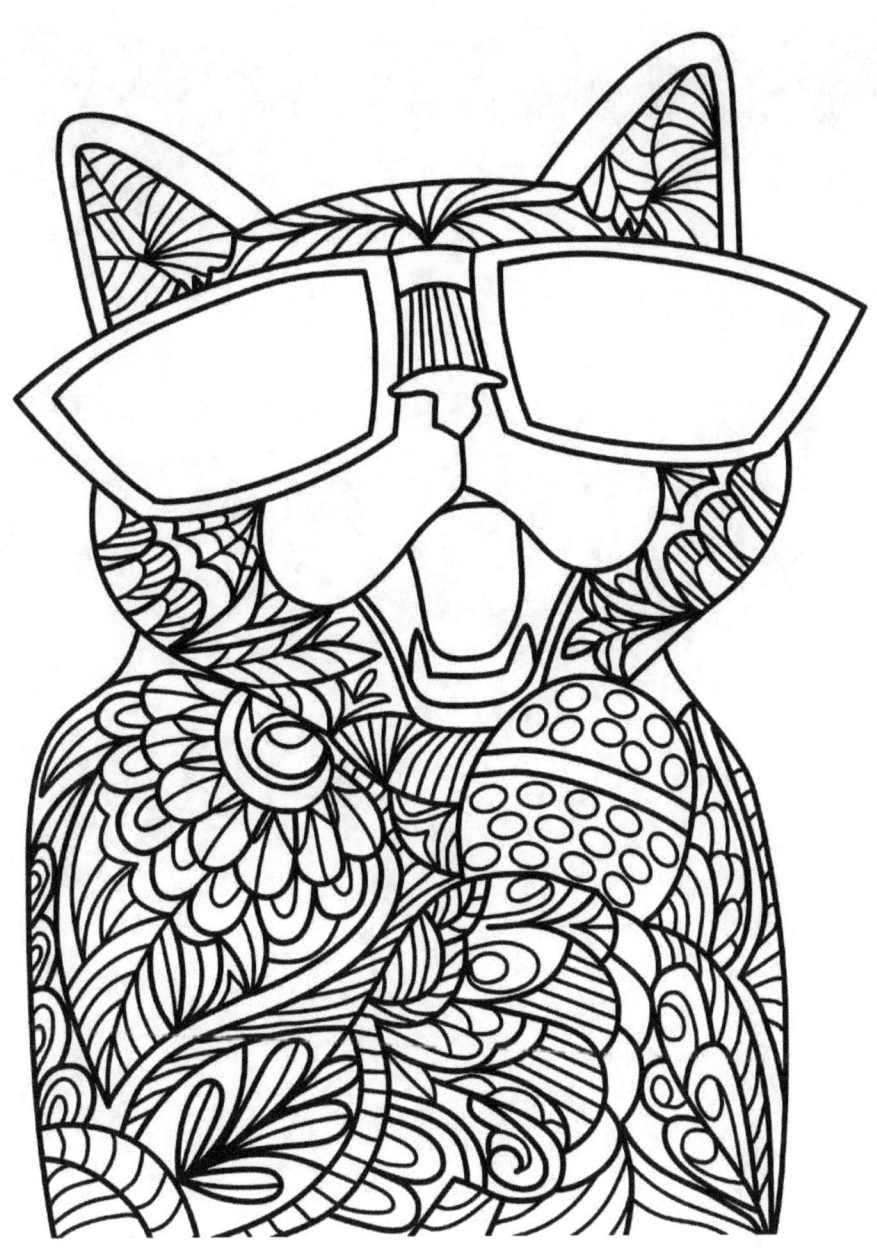

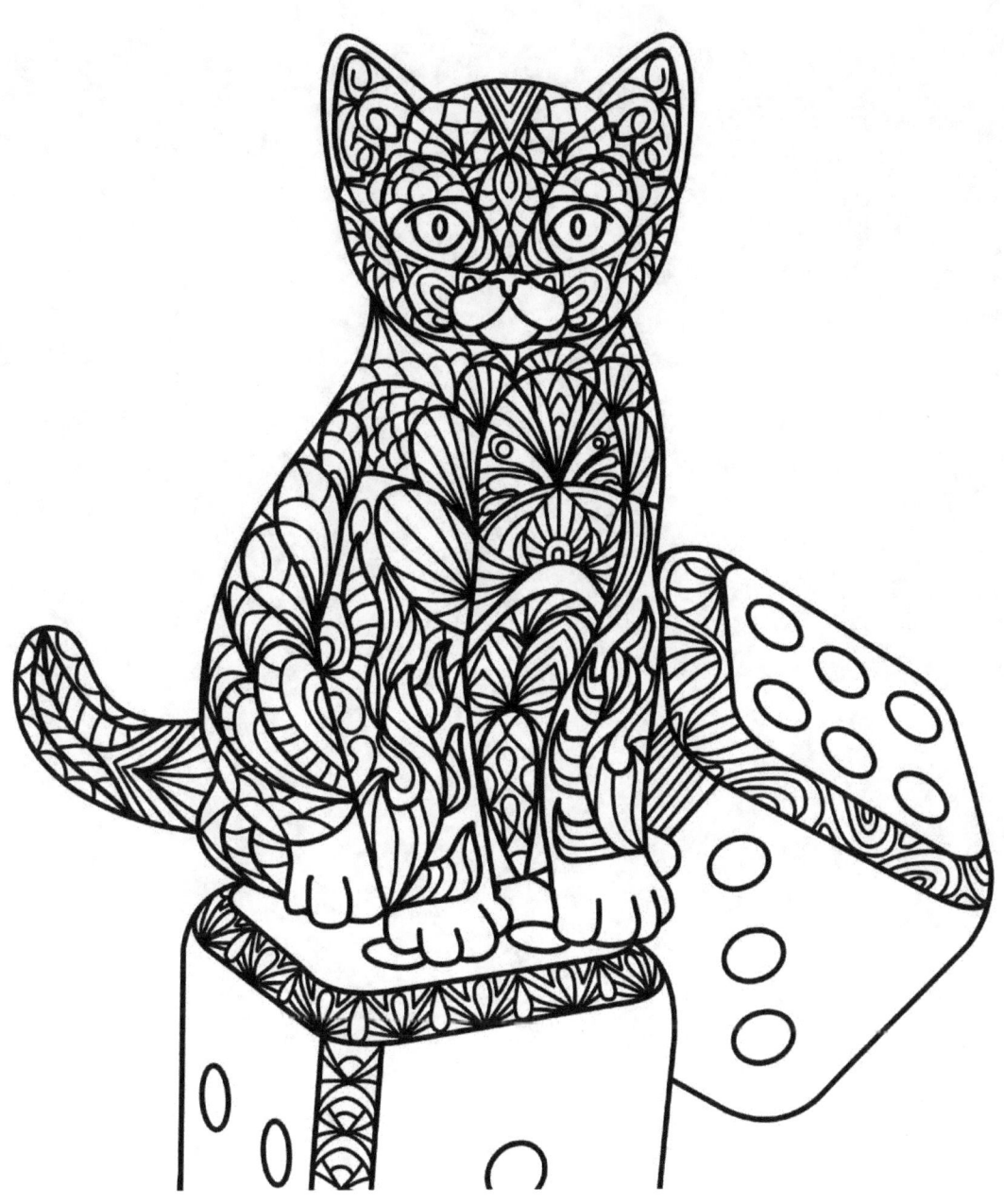

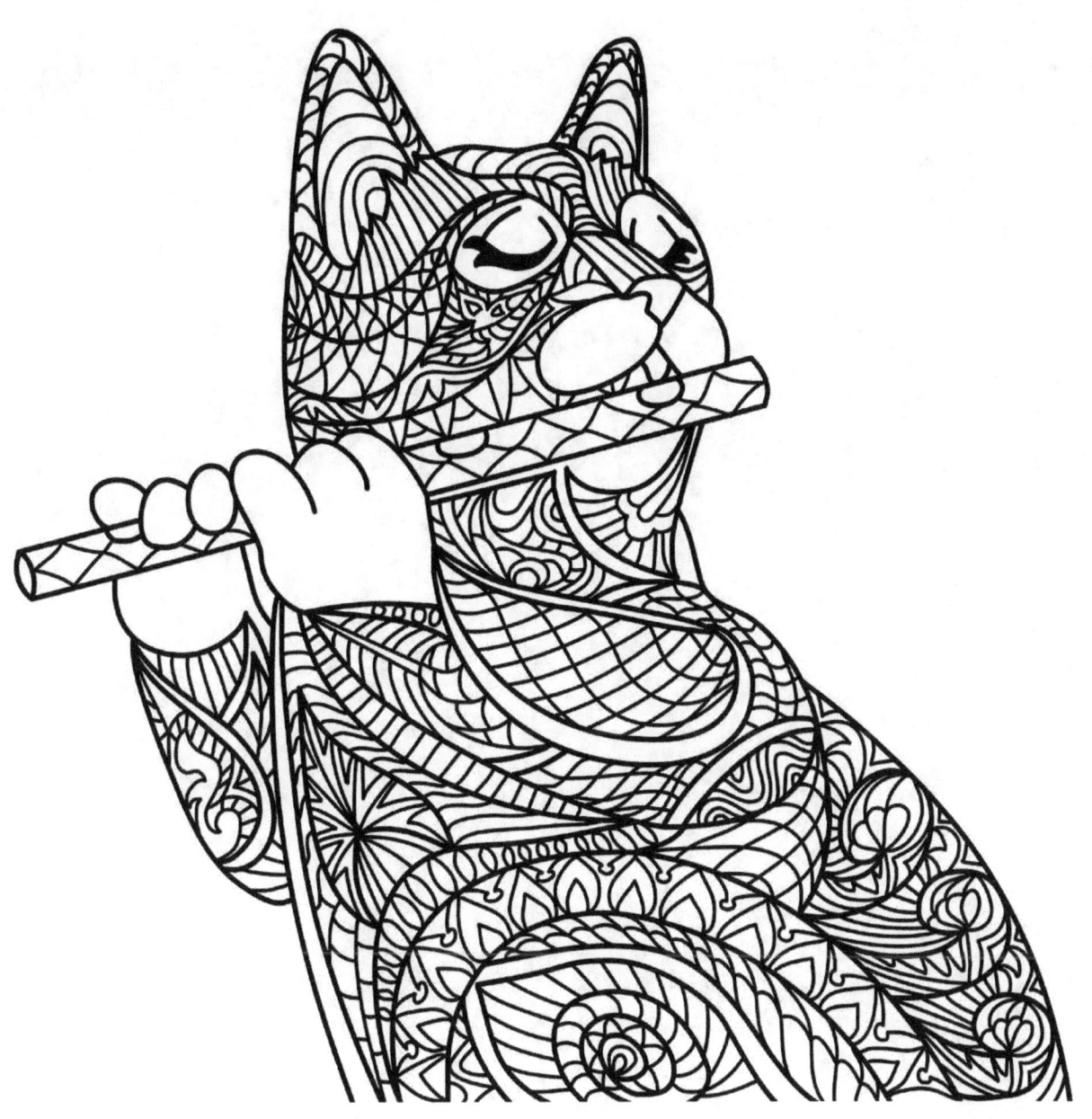

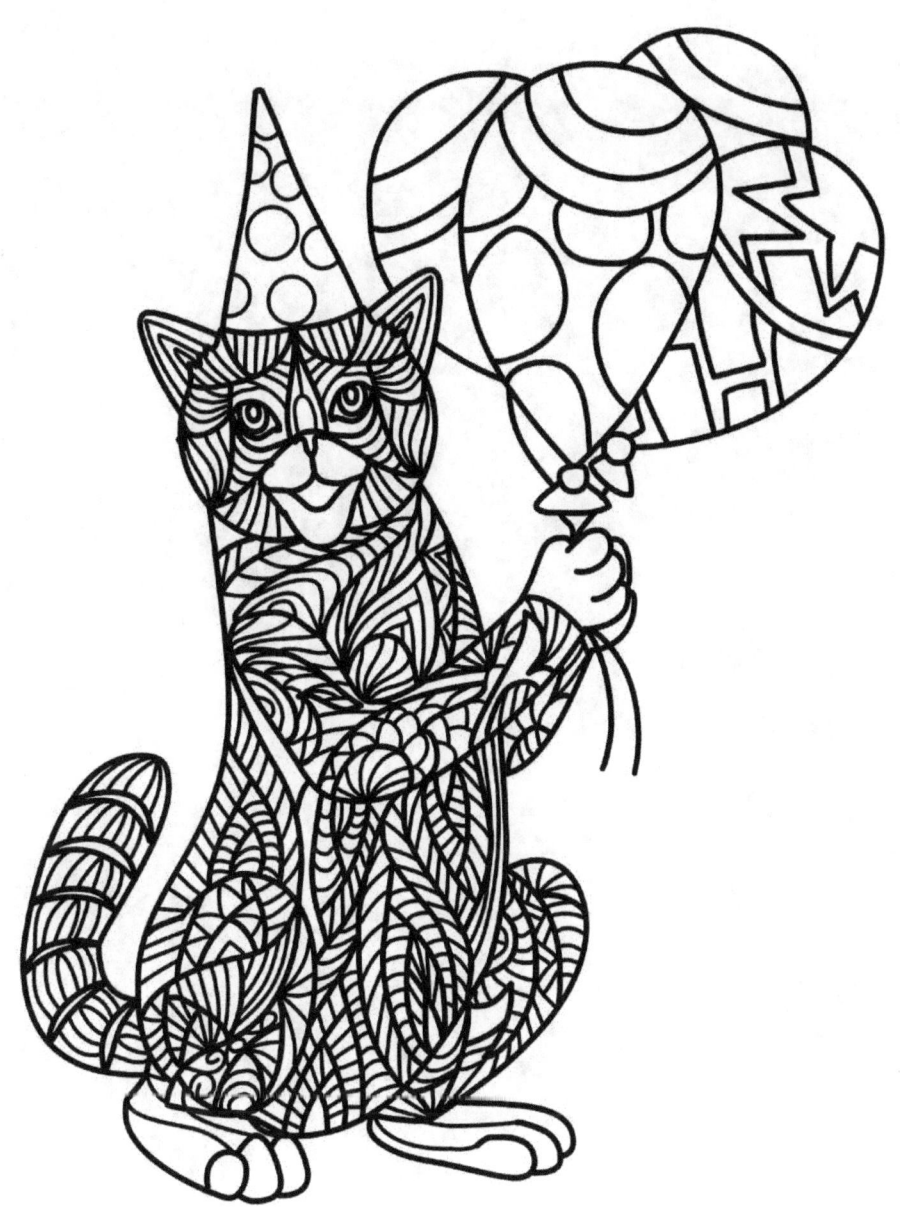

www.ingramcontent.com/pod-product-compliance
Lightning Source LLC
Chambersburg PA
CBHW080922170526
45158CB00008B/2206